# GOOGLE ADWORDS

A Beginner's Guide to BOOST YOUR BUSINESS

Use Google Analytics, SEO Optimization, YouTube and Ads

# Contents

# Description

Google Marketing is a powerful showcasing approach for business owners. You can show your product or service promotion to potential customers searching for your type of solution. Secondly, you can target people searching exactly where you are located. This makes most business owners have to promote on Google necessarily.

## Everything About Google AdWords

Google AdWords is a solution that can take your business to the following degree. You can place and run promotions displayed with an exact Googles search. These promotions will look smooth as well as attractive in their appearances. Google sets these advertisements tactically above, beside, or below the search results web page when individuals look for your keywords.

When a purchaser looks for a term or expression, Google will undoubtedly reveal crucial discounts depending on the keywords used in the query to the client. Websites that need their coupons to show up on the results web page deal on keyword expressions that they rely upon. People will undoubtedly utilize these keywords when looking for their kind of organization. For instance, a handyman placed in Atlanta may depend on the search phrases such as "woodworking Florida," "Home timber products," or "woodwork devices."

Contingent upon the amount you offer contrasted with different handypersons in the area, your promotion may appear on the outcomes web page when individuals check for the terms you provide. No matter the amount you give, Google additionally considers the importance along with the nature of your advertisement and the website. So regardless of whether you have one of the most fantastic products or services, the promo for your shop will most likely never show up in search when someone looks for "labor residence work."

You need to have a great deal of certainty with essential expressions.

This guide will focus on the following:

- Choosing Keywords
- How To Build A Google Friendly Website
- Local SEO Begins at Home
- Website Content that is Keyword Specific
- Creating Compelling Ads
- Optimizing for Conversions
- Tips on Improving your Content Marketing Strategy
- Search Campaigns Ad Group Settings & structure
- Converting Your Followers
- How to Optimize Your AdWords Campaign… AND MORE!!!

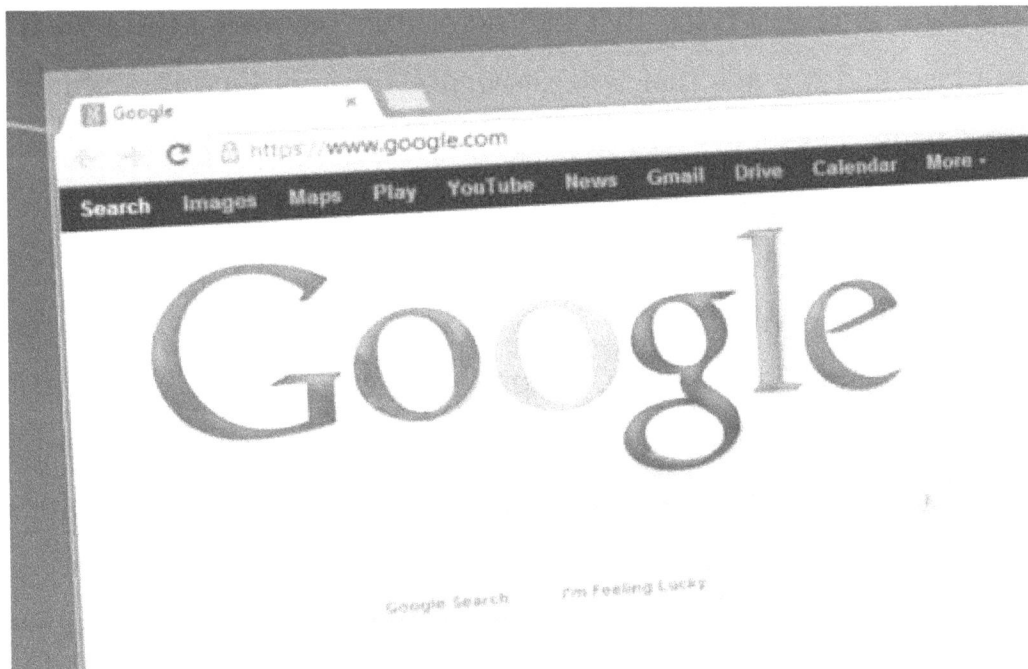

# Introduction

Most haven't given much thought to Gmail, Google Plus, and AdWords regarding social media marketing. Your business could be passing up some essential advantages.

Over the most recent couple of years, Gmail has experienced some significant updates, including enabling organizations to interface with clients and prospects. This chapter will give you a short introduction on all that you have to think about when it comes to Gmail and Google Plus and how to use them as a great tool to boost your brand's image.

Google promoting is an extraordinary showcasing technique for entrepreneurs. You can show promotion for your business to individuals hunting down your kind of business at that exact second and who are searching for organizations in your vicinity. This kind of focusing makes most entrepreneurs need to publicize on Google.

**All About Google AdWords**

Google Adwords is a service that can take your business to the next level. You can place and run ads that will showcase right on Google's search, even on the first page. These ads will pop up and look smooth and catchy. Google places these ads strategically at either the top or bottom of their page when people search your keyword.

**How Ads on Google Work**

When a buyer scans for a term or expression, Google will demonstrate the essential customer promotions dependent on the keywords utilized in the inquiry. Sites that need their advertisements to appear on the outcomes page offer keywords they trust. Individuals will use these keywords when searching for their sort of business. For instance, a handyman situated in Atlanta may offer the keywords such as "woodworking Florida," "Home wood materials," or "woodwork tools."

Depending on the amount you offer compared to competitors in your territory, your advertisement may or may not appear on the results page when individuals search with the words you target. Notwithstanding the amount you offer, Google additionally considers the significance and nature of your advertisement and site. So regardless of whether you have the most astounding delivered, the ad for your store will presumably never show up in search when somebody seeks "labor housework." You have to be more specific with keywords.

**The Benefits of Advertising on Google**

There are three essential advantages to promoting on Google:

1. Searchers are Committed to Buying

Individuals seeking Google are ordinarily in the market for the catchphrases they are hunting down. If someone is looking for a "smart TV," it makes it impossible to expect they are searching for a store to buy T-shirts soon after that. You can ensure that only individuals in your close area see your promotion because you may set the geographic area where you need your advertisement to appear. For instance, you can advise Google to advertise to California individuals.

Contrast this with promoting on Facebook. Even though you can advertise your t-shirts to somebody who is a known cool shirt fan, you have to focus on those searching for a place to buy shirts.

These are the reasons that make publicizing on Google so effective and dissimilar to other promoting. You are explicitly focusing on individuals in the market for your products or service. Not just that, you can target just individuals situated in your general vicinity, which is a tremendous addition to nearby organizations.

2. You Won't Pay Unless Customers Click on The Ads You Create

Another alluring variable is that you pay if your notice works. Since Google utilizes compensation for every snap publicizing model, you spend on the off chance that somebody is scanning for the watchword you have offered on and is intrigued enough in your promotion to tap on it.

You can set the amount you will pay per tap on your advertisement and choose an appropriate day-by-day spending plan. This is the big difference between google advertising and a simple newspaper ad that costs a standard value regardless of whether someone takes a look at your ad or not.

Google AdWords has changed how publicizes work by just making you pay when the client has made a move to see your site. We will expound the amount it expenses later in the article.

## 3. Live Tracking for Your Ads

With the AdWords dashboard, you can follow what number of individuals see your promotion, the number of taps on your advertisement, and what number of make a move once on your site. That way, on the off chance that you see that many individuals are tapping on your advertisement, yet nobody is purchasing anything once on your site, you realize you have to alter either the greeting page or the promotion itself. By keeping a heartbeat on how your advertisement is getting along, you can rapidly make any essential changes with the end goal of an effective promotion campaign.

The following abilities with publicizing on Google are colossal for independent companies. Envision your flower shop and choose to purchase a board ad. Unless the client lets you know, there would be practically no data letting you know whether anybody went to your store since they saw the announcement. You would make a significant venture without knowing whether it yielded a positive return.

With Google advertisements, you can follow precisely how many individuals visited your site since they tapped on your promotion. There is a minor hazard since you can quit running an ad because you are not getting the outcomes you need anytime you see that. We will investigate the ideal approaches to follow your promotions later in the article.

## How Google Analyzes Where Your Ads are Placed

Google utilizes a mix of three essential variables to decide when a promotion appears on the outcomes page:

**Offer:** The offer is the value you will pay for a tick on your promotion. You offer against the different sites on watchwords you trust individuals scan for, for the off chance they are interested in your item. A home business store may provide the expressions "startup home based business" or "make money online" or "Forex Trading at Home."

**Quality and pertinence of the advertisement:** Your promotion should have the ultimate goal of appearing on the indexed listings page. On the off chance that somebody seeks "business ideas", it wouldn't bode well for Google to demonstrate an advertisement for a Target department store. You need to make sure that you have several slogans so that Google can consider your promotion as meaningful for hunting.

**Presentation page understanding:** When someone taps your advertisement, the greeting page sent to them should have content comparable to the promotion itself and contain the words used in the ad. Suppose you have a salon and are promoting nail trims. In that case, you'll need to connect straightforwardly to a page that has more data on nail trims rather than to the landing page, which incorporates the majority of your administrations.

Portable and work area promotions on Google are fundamentally the same. They are both presentation advertisements at the best and base of the query items page, and you offer on watchwords a similar route with both. Even though some entrepreneurs neglect versatility, it is something you unquestionably need to consider when promoting on Google. The most significant portion of Google's enterprise is cell phones, and individuals searching on their cell phones regularly have nearby options.

The critical contrasts among work area and portable promoting are:

- There is less space on a smartphone, so you have to ensure your message is direct to the point.
- Individuals on their phones are in a hurry, so you need to tailor your message for the precise lifestyle.

gleeful keen thrilled blessed tender excited
relaxed anxious affected reliable bold elated
gay animated hopeful courageous cheerful friskybright
loving pleased wonderful devoted nosy OPEN curious
and re-enforced jubilant liberated receptive dynamic
sympathy affectionate overjoyed important festive
tenacious satisfied enthusiastic admiration
spirited close INTERESTED understanding hardy
loved impulsive HAPPY confident
sensitive comforted daring quiet
delighted challenged earnest joyous STRONG provocative encouraged
sure optimistic sunny intrigued merry passionate
LOVE sympathetic snoopy POSITIVE ease engrossed intent
unique peaceful easy certain comfortable determined
drawn challenged accepting ALIVE considerate surprised rebellious inquisitive
great calm thankful lucky inspired GOOD kind concerned energetic amazed brave reassured serene
ecstatic fortunate absorbed content
attracted free playful eager secure
clever touched warm glad
toward

# Chapter 1 - Choosing Keywords

Imagine being stranded out at sea with no mode of communication. That is how it feels when you have a business no one is aware of except you and your staff, of course. Google Local is the best resource if you want your target audience to locate your local business online quickly. People are more likely to find your company via Google than if you deploy traditional offline marketing techniques.

Google will not automatically project your business to your intended target. You will have to help Google grow your business with the right keywords or phrases. These keywords or phrases play a significant role in ensuring that your business gets an impressive ranking on Google and other famous search engines.

Your intended target audience will search for businesses such as yours using specific keywords or phrases. To rank high on Google so that your target audience can quickly locate your business, you will have to incorporate these local keywords or phrases on your Google My Business Listing and in the web content on your website. Not all companies are ranked in localized web searches, even though this may seem simple enough.

Website owners have no idea how to find those keywords or phrases that will help their business to rank high in localized web searches by their target audience. The question to be asked at this point is: can local keywords or phrases be found?

Well, there are different ways to find local keywords or phrases that would help get your business ranked up on search engines like Google. You can learn how to locate these keywords in this chapter.

**Search Engines Now Personalize Search Results**

Google works assiduously to have search results personalized as much as possible, and this is in stark contrast to what was obtained some time back. The top five or so search results in one state in the U.S, for example, would also be the top five search results in another state. This has dramatically changed the way businesses search for the ideal keywords or phrases that will help them rank high on search engines.

These days Google deploys a localized technique. When a person uses specific keywords or phrases on Google in search of a business, the businesses closest to the person and those listed in local directories are given top priority.

Google will pinpoint the person's location searching and then return those businesses that are closest to their location. Google also personally provides individuals logged into their respective Google accounts with localized search results.

**How to Choose Localized Keywords and Phrases**

If you want to locate local keywords or phrases to help your business rank high on Google and other search engines, you can use three easy steps today.

The first step you should consider in choosing localized keywords or phrases is to locate industry-standard keywords or phrases.

**1. Locate Industry Standard Keywords**

People regularly use keywords or phrases when searching online for a business. Your objective will be to find out those ranking keywords or phrases used by people when they want to describe your respective local business. You need to think the same way as your target audience and contemplate what keywords or phrases might be used when searching for your business on Google. Come up with a comprehensive list comprising of about ten local business keywords or phrases.

A typical local standard keyword or phrase list for a "vaporizer pen business" could include the following; "vape pen" or "vape pen business."

## 2. Locate and Make Use of Modifiers

When people are searching for a business on Google or any other search engine, they usually use modifiers. With modifiers, people may find a specific business or commodity. Modifiers are those words or phrases that will further describe a company to enhance a search result. Some modifiers examples in the case of the "vaporizer pen business" are:

- "wax vaporizer pen"
- "CBD vaporizer pen"
- "dry herb vaporizer pen"
- "the best vaporizer pen"
- "pink striped vaporizer pen"
- "cheapest vaporizer pen"

## 3. Use Local Specific Keywords or Phrases

The final step in choosing keywords or phrases that could help your business rank high on Google Local includes specific locations.

If your business intends to provide commodities for people of an area or region, you will have to use location-specific keywords. These keywords could be used by people in narrowing down their search results to businesses within their locality.

The content of your website would need to have locations as keywords to help with your ranking on search engines. The truth is, your target audience would most likely be looking for those businesses closest.

Still, going back to the example of a "vaporizer pen business," you may want to limit or specify the locality of the vaporizer pen being searched for. For example, "vaporizer pen in Detroit," "Long Island vape pen," or "vaporizer pen L.A." This way, your business would rank high on local search results by people (your target audience) in your area of business.

# Chapter 2 - Local SEO Begins at Home

What you need to promote your local business online is "out there," meaning it's not part of your website.

But not yet. Not until you've done what needs doing to your website. See, Local SEO happens in two places: on-site (on your website) and off-site (everywhere else on the Internet). You may also hear this referred to as on-page SEO and off-page SEO.

Once you've got your on-site situation squared away, it will be a lot easier to handle the off-site tasks. Without proper on-site SEO, your website will never be able to reach its local ranking potential. Once you get it right, your site will be working for you instead of just wallowing in the search engine abyss.

The heart of SEO is to know how to choose and use the right keywords.

## What Is a Keyword?

It is the word, or phrase people key into a search engine like Google when they search for something. Occasionally, it is called a key phrase when more than one word is used. But whether it's a phrase or a word, it's usually referred to as a keyword. Keywords form the basis for all Search Engine Optimization strategies, so before you ramp up your SEO program, you must know which keywords your prospective customers are using when searching for your products and services.

## Probable-Keyword Tools & Selecting the Right Keywords

As it turns out, there are some free tools you can use to help develop a list of probable keywords. The most popular is Google's Keyword Planner. This is a tool for Google's pay-per-click (PPC) service, AdWords. However, it's a great free tool that you can use for SEO keyword research:

https://adwords.google.com/KeywordPlanner

Just type in a word or phrase that you think people might use when searching for you. The tool will kick out a list of associated keywords with information about the number of searches done for each keyword per month. It also indicates the competitiveness of each keyword, meaning how many other companies are engaging in a PPC bidding war for a given word or phrase. This is handy information because if the volume, suggested price per click, and the competition level is high, you know that those keywords correlate to more sales, and thus those are the terms and phrases you should focus on. Proper keyword research takes the guesswork out of SEO.

The following picture shows an example for the search of "plumbing" that generate 717 keywords idea available:

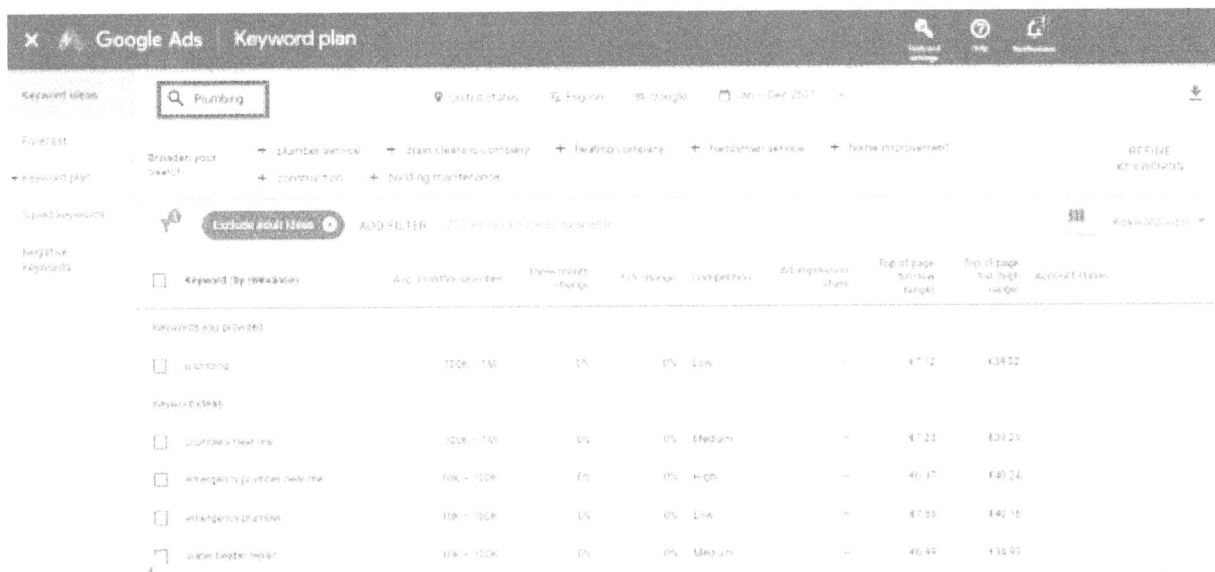

## Long-Tail Keywords

Naturally, shorter, more generic words and phrases have more competition than longer, more specific keywords, called "long-tail" keywords. The more detailed a long-tail keyword is, the easier it is for your website to rank when people search for it. As a local business owner, you'll be happy to learn that local long-tail keywords – like "Plumbing Supplies Atlanta, GA" – appear in over 40% of all Google searches. Using the counties, cities, or neighborhoods your company services in your local SEO program can radically improve their effectiveness. In other words, you'll want to naturally use various combinations of [city or suburb] + [service] in your web page and blog copy, as well as the other SEO-related website code on your site (more on that later).

After you've finished your keyword research, you should have scores of potential keywords that might be used by searchers looking for what your company provides. Sounds like a lot, right? Well, it's not. Think about all the possible terms people might use to search for what you do.

For example, here's a list of keywords for an Atlanta, GA plumbing company:

- Atlanta GA Plumbing Company
- Atlanta GA Plumbing Repair
- Atlanta GA Plumbing Service
- Atlanta GA Commercial Plumbing
- Atlanta GA Residential Plumbing
- Plumbing Company Atlanta GA
- Plumbing Repair Atlanta GA
- Plumbing Service Atlanta GA
- Commercial Plumbing Atlanta GA
- Residential Plumbing Atlanta GA

And that's just the beginning. It's not even counting other terms like toilet repair, septic system, garbage disposal, sump pump, water heater, etc. And of course, there are more specific geographic references for areas around Atlanta like Alpharetta, Marietta, Peachtree City, and Athens. Once you start adding in these combinations of variables, the list explodes.

Ok, so now you've got a list of a couple of hundred possible keywords. What should you do with them?

## Your Keywords, Your Website

When you look at your website, examine it closely, page by page. Choose one to two keywords per page, and optimize that page for that keyword(s), including your home page.

As you write the content for that page, be sure to include your keyword in a few different places on the page, including:

**The page title:** this is the browser bar title on your site, and usually see the blue clickable title text in search engine results.

**The meta tag (meta description):** This text is not visible on your website, but it's typically the text you see under the blue title text within Google search results.

**Image ALT tags and title tags for any images on your page:** Google cannot read graphic text, so you can use computer code to assign a keyword or phrase to every image on your site, so Google knows the context of the image and its relevance to the web page.

**Anchor links:** Anywhere throughout your text, you include a clickable link to another page on your website. If you mention one product or service on a page, make a clickable link to that product or service and use your keyword as the clickable anchor text.

**Geo-targeted phrases:** Anytime your text includes naturally geo-targeted phrases (like city, neighborhood, or suburbs) on a web page or in a blog post.

**Outbound Global Authority Links:** Whenever you include a clickable link to an authority site in your industry (this is good to do!), providing that it adds value and is relevant to the content on a given page.

Outbound Local Authority Links Whenever you include a clickable link to a local website (Chamber of Commerce, a local government site, or a local news site), again – providing its natural, relevant. It adds editorial value to the page or blog post.

Make sure you don't just stick your keywords anywhere to help your SEO efforts. You should only insert them where they fit naturally, add to the content flow, and make editorial sense. As helpful as keywords are to your website, "stuffing" words and links to and from your website can be equally damaging to your website. Google, in particular, is excellent at sniffing out websites that over-optimize or use manipulative SEO techniques to try and game their system. If you stick to quality content that naturally works in keyword phrases into your website, you should not have to worry about search engine penalties. Google has a detailed list of quality guidelines you can find here:

https://support.google.com/webmasters/answer/35769

The anchor text link is built directly into the text rather than a traditional URL link. For example, if the text says "List of our plumbing supplies" and you made that phrase a clickable link, that would be an example of an anchor text link. It is quite different and much more common today than telling your website visitors, "For more information on our plumbing supplies, visit www.atlantaplumbinginc.com/supplies." Compared to the traditional URL link, you can see how cleaner the anchor text link is.

Regarding linking out to other sites, your website visitors might find it helpful if you link to other websites that might add some contextual value to that page's content, like to a "Who's Who in Plumbing" website. And it's not just to jack up your value with the search engines. Your website visitors will also appreciate it if you have these kinds of links to authoritative resource websites. Simply put, these outbound links improve the website's overall content, and that's always a good thing.

Next, you'll need to duplicate this procedure for every page on your website.

Of course, you'll need to do it again whenever you add a new page or a blog post, which you should be doing regularly to enhance your ranking.

**Don't Skimp on Content**

It's essential to make sure every page on your website has "enough" text to gain the respect of the search engines as a legitimate, valuable page. Part of determining how a search engine views your pages' value involves how long visitors stay on those pages. If you've got just a little bit of text, they'll read it in seconds and click elsewhere. That's not good.

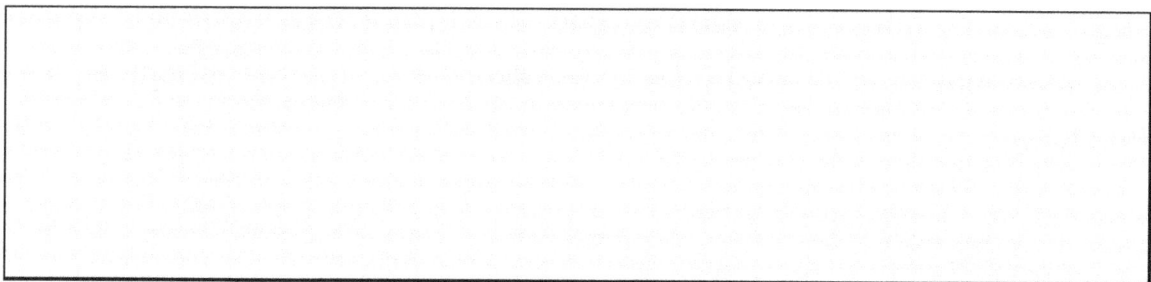

You want enough words on your pages to say what you need to say, to engage your readers, and to make them stay put for more than ten seconds. Here are some guidelines for content length:

- Home page: 200-300 words
- Core service pages: 300+ words
- Blog posts: 500+ words minimum

Long-form or in-depth blog posts: blog posts of 1,000 to 2,500 words or more are performing better on the search engines these days.

Be sure the text on every page is accessible to the eyes. No overwhelming blocks of text. No super-long paragraphs. Use sub-headlines, bullet points, embedded YouTube videos images to make the page appealing.

**Go Mobile!**

The statistics on mobile usage are staggering. Over 50% of all searches are from mobile devices. The odds are good that when your new customers look for you online, they're using a smartphone or a tablet. If your website isn't mobile-friendly in a mobile responsive design, you're sunk! They'll click to your competitor's mobile responsive site and forget all about you.

There's a saying about mobile: "Pinch and zoom spell your doom." What it means is that if your smartphone-using website visitors can't navigate and use your website (and read what's on it) without having to use their fingers to expand and move your content, you've got a severe problem. In other words: "Thumb-scroll to get the cash to roll!"

When mobile sites first became popular, many companies set up separate websites for desktop and smartphone users. These sites would somehow recognize which machine the user was on and send them to the appropriate venue. That's an old hat now.

Now, the technology is called responsive. It's the same in that it detects whether a visitor is on a desktop or a mobile device, but there is no longer any need for a separate website. Thank goodness, because, with two sites, you face double the trouble for optimization tasks!

Not sure whether your website is responsive? Whip out your smartphone and take a look. Can you read and use your site without squinting or doing the old pinch and zoom?

Want a more scientific way to know whether your website is mobile-friendly? Just enter your website into this tool, and you'll find out whether Google thinks it is:

https://www.google.com/webmasters/tools/mobile-friendly/

### Introducing The Grand Schema

Every project has that one phase that's just awful. If you're painting, it's the wall prep. If you're sewing, it's pinning the pattern. If you're building a paver patio, it's tamping the ground.

If you're optimizing your website, it's Schema. It's pretty much a guarantee that you won't want to do this step – but we'd be doing you no favors by not telling you about it.

Schema markup is a way to make your website easier for search engines to find. It tells search engines what your website means instead of what it says. That's every bit as important as it sounds.

Essentially Schema is a format (AKA whole other foreign, techy language) you apply to the HTML code of your web pages to give the search engines the information they need to identify your content. The Schema microdata is what forms rich snippets of your content, which ends up on the search engine results page. (Yes, we know, it hurts!) A typical example is when you see extra information in search results, such as a product star rating or event listings. Schema is a unique SEO code that tells Google you want to consider showing this extra information to searchers.

Categorizing your content well is critical to the search engines' ability to serve relevant information when people search. Irrelevant content in the search engine results is the surest way to lose users, which translates to billions of dollars in lost revenue.

So, for you, Schema's significant pain in the neck, the likes of which we can't adequately convey. For search engines, Schema's a considerable hurdle. They want to watch you jump when they serve up your site to searchers who will quickly see that they're in the right place.

Even without stepping into Schema, the entire on-site optimization process is time-consuming, not to mention complicated, especially if you've got a decent-sized website. That's why reputable Local SEO agencies find that their clients are eager to hand this set of tasks off to them.

OK, that part is over. We apologize in advance for any Schema-themed nightmares you have tonight. It has to be done, but it sure isn't pleasant.

Next up, we'll zero in on how Local SEO works and what you need to know if you want to remain competitive in your location. While most business owners have a passing understanding of 'regular' SEO, the local business owners who grasp Local SEO are the ones who get a steady stream of new customers coming in.

# Chapter 3 -PPC vs. SEO

First, let's understand the differences between ads and organic SEO results. When Google shows a search result, we must remember that paid ads appear above organic search results. The former is PPC, which has to be paid for by the advertiser, such as Jorge or Sophia. On the other hand, the latter is free but requires time to get right-SEO. Implementing SEO strategies to increase your organic ranking in Google does not cost a dollar but will take time away from your business or enterprise. Both Jorge and Sophia need to do some back-end calculations to determine which strategy works best. For example, if Jorge finds that artwork for advertisements never really sells well, he may opt for a strong SEO strategy. On the other hand, if Sophia can obtain a strong CPC ratio in her PPC, she may choose to go the advertisement route.

Besides the relatively low costs associated with SEO, there are a few other benefits. A strong SEO strategy creates awareness within Google of your company or business, but this is a double-edged sword. One bad review can stay at the top of your Google rankings for a long time. Instead, a string of good reviews can bolster user confidence in your product. This confidence builds upon credibility and trust. A small business like the one running Sophia needs to rely on more repeat customers, which means the better their reviews, the more profits Sophia can generate. In that sense, if Sophia sees that her small business is climbing the Google rankings, she's already miles ahead of many other vendors in the same industry. That said, being miles ahead of the competition takes a lot of extra hard work.

So, what if you don't have much competition in your field? Specific industries are hyper-geographically focused, such as wedding photographers, for example. Few wedding photographers are interested in traveling across the country to cover a wedding. This means that if you're a wedding photographer living in the Tulsa suburbs, you probably don't have too much competition. So, when someone in Tulsa searches for "wedding photographers near me" or "wedding photography in Tulsa", your page is more likely to reach the top of the Google rankings. The wedding photographer should employ a targeted SEO strategy rather than struggling and paying for PPC if this is the case.

First, if you are looking to employ an SEO strategy, you need to consider that you will be competing with giants like Amazon and eBay. If you see that your site is consistently ranking lower than these titans, you may need to re-think your strategy (perhaps selling Sophia candles on Etsy could do the trick).

Some businesses offer a unique product, such as Jorge's vintage prints of Chicago. These can't be found anywhere else but Curious Jorge's. Because of this, he does not have to compete with Amazon, eBay, or Craigslist. On the other hand, there are multiple vendors of soy-based candles, meaning that Sophia's competition in her niche is much stronger. Again, choosing SEO or PPC depends on your business model.

PPC offers a very targeted audience. Because of this, you're not competing with Amazon or eBay, who sell everything, but rather another very niche market. This highly targeted audience may be smaller but much more receptive to paid ads in their results since they searched for just that! Another benefit of PPC is time. While developing website credibility and increasing Google rank takes a long time, creating a paid ad can take a day. Using PPC in this way can be a great way to quickly increase your online visibility, especially if you want to sell products during vacations or Valentine's Day. Again, this really depends on your business model. Concerning the speed of posting your products, PPC is a good strategy if a business owner is testing a product to see how successful it can be. Since you get results relatively quickly, there are more ways to test the product and measure its popularity.

Here's another great thing about PPC. Contrary to SEO strategies that pit one website against another, PPC represents graphically the product you're selling. If you sell a visual attractive product, PPC may be exactly the strategy for you, especially if it is a unique product. If you are a woodworker trying to sell 2x4s, a PPC approach is maybe not for you because 2x4s are not visually appealing. However, if your small business does design handmade pens, PPC is a more viable strategy now, as these can appear as visually appealing ads on Google. PPC is also a good strategy if you are a modest company that sells several different items. While all candles may look more or less the same, if you are a jeweler with many kinds of necklaces, earrings, bracelets, and rings, then you are consistently pumping out new products and product lines. This would render PPC a more potent strategy than SEO because otherwise, users would have to search for specific keywords to reach your landing page.

As the reader may remember from above, using PPC and SEO is costly (PPC) and time-consuming (SEO). If the entrepreneur has changed strategies or is looking to get a product off the ground quickly, then an oscillation between PPC for the new product, combined with SEO later on, could be a great idea. Once users start searching for the product online more frequently, the entrepreneur can remove the paid ads. Then, when there is another product they wish to sell, they can repeat the process ad infinitum. Here's the trick to this strategy: the entrepreneur must switch systems repeatedly. This method works if a business is selling different products or growing at such as fast rate that a new product line is ordered every few months.

Some readers may be tempted to use both SEO and PPC simultaneously. This is possible, but unless you have a special reason, it is typically not considered an excellent strategy. Not only does this tactic cost time and money, but your efforts may also finally cancel each other out. Imagine if a user searches for soy candles online and sees a website organically found through SEO techniques and an ad for the same product placed through PPC. Sophia's best interest is that the user clicks through to its website and saves the cost of click-through advertising, but this is not a guarantee. Ultimately, having your webpage pop up twice for one search cuts the effectiveness of both strategies by half, rendering this combination a suboptimal solution to online marketing problems.

By now, the reader should be familiar with the differences between PPC and SEO and have a general idea of what strategy they would be using for their business. We have purposefully been putting off the second part of SEO— branding. This next section discusses how branding can develop your SEO strategy over time.

## Website Content that is Keyword Specific

Once you have determined the website layout, you are ready to start researching keywords and keyword phrases. Your keywords directly relate to the user intention and your overall target audience. Suppose you target the older population, such as anyone in their 60s and older. In that case, your language will need to reflect your target audience by being more formal than trying to attract teenagers. The keywords also have to relate to age. Do you think someone in their 70s would understand ROFL in a text unless it was explained to them on a previous occasion? It is like some urban slang that better fits a younger target audience.

Google has become a powerhouse of intelligence. The algorithms can search for specific keywords, tell you others are missing, and display relevant results. But, how do you find the keywords you need? Do you make them up and hope for the best?

Yes, and no, what you sell provides general keywords. There are keyword tools to find broad and niche terms for your website content to target your audience better. You will begin a keyword search based on what you sell.

## Use Google Keyword Tools

Google has AdWords, which is a keyword search tool. It was designed explicitly for creating a banner and pay-per-click ads. However, you can also run a keyword search to determine which words are most famous for your sell items. There are other keyword tools, but since you are targeting Google, it is best to stick with AdWords.

The keyword planner can help you find new keywords and see the search volume data. According to the Google AdWords search page, you can search for new keywords using a phrase, website, or category. You can also search for trends and volume data, as well as multiply keywords as a way to get new keywords.

First, choose to search for new keywords based on a category, website, or phrase. You can enter your product or service and customize your search for the best results. Let's use pets as an example again.

The results will appear in ad group ideas. If you used pet, you might see pet adoption, pet shop, dog adoption, puppy, pet supplies, cat, online store as the ad group ideas. You can also click to get a list of keyword ideas. You will care about two columns in the displayed results: average monthly searches and competition.

The average monthly searches tell you how frequently online users use the specific keyword or keyword phrase. For pets, the average number of monthly searches is 60,500. The competition is considered low, meaning there are not a lot of companies trying to buy that word and use it in their ads. Dogs are searched for 673,000 times, and the competition is low because it is not specific enough to create an ad.

## You want Broad and Niche Keywords

As you generate keyword lists, not only to assess the frequency they are used in a search, but whether there is a high competition for the word, you need to find two types of keywords.

Pets, pet, dog, dogs, and pet supplies are broad terms. Any site that sells items relating to any pet will use these broad terms. They do so for word flow. You must use dog when you are talking about the dog. This is why the competition for the word is low in ads.

What if you used dog supplies in Cleveland, such as "We sell dog supplies in Cleveland at our…?" You have just narrowed dog supplies to a specific niche. You tell an online user that your store is located in Cleveland, and because they live in Cleveland, Google displayed results based on their location.

They didn't even have to use the keyword phrase "dog supplies Cleveland" to get your webpage. Google tracks your location and determines the best results based on where you live or your most typical searches for specific areas helps get you the local results.

If you sell only organic pet supplies, you would want to use organic in your website content and avoid using terms like non-organic or leaving off organic.

## Do not Misspell Words

It is tantalizing to misspell words to attract a varied target audience. However, Google has improved its intelligence, and you no longer need to misspell words. Google will display two types of results:

- Showing results for "correctly spelled words"
- Search instead for "incorrectly spelled words"

Google will ask you if you meant to spell the word correctly and wanted those results or if you liked it spelled the other way. For example, if you typed in "trafing online" google will show up results for "trading online" on the assumption that you meant trading and not a non-existent word "trafing".

## Keywords in Headings and Subheadings

Each page will have a heading or a title. This heading needs to have your main keyword—the word you know will be searched and put your website on the first page of the Google rankings. It is the niche keyword. Your subheadings or H2 headings also need to have keywords. These keywords should relate to the page topic and the niche keyword you are targeting for that page. For example, an H2 heading might be girl's clothing, sizes 5-14. This way, if someone is searching for those clothing sizes for girls, they will find the right page in the Google page results.

If the keyword appears in the headings and subheadings, it must also appear in the written content on that page.

# Chapter 4 - Writing the Website Content

You are ready to write your content based on SEO practices. You have your website layout designed for a user-friendly experience. You grabbed keyword lists to determine what people search for, understanding the broad and niche keywords that will help your site land on the first page of Google search results.

You need to create the website content, the actual words, and images to fill the page with appropriate internal links. Remember, Google sends out search bots that will index your website pages, allowing your page to display in the results when someone searches for the keywords or topic of your pages.

For the bots to search your content, you need external links that bring a person to your site and internal links that help a user navigate your website.

## Write Naturally

Do not try to force keywords into your written work. Your content should be without mistakes, grammatically correct, and flow naturally. Your target audience will know if something is confusing due to improper flow or grammatical errors. Nothing has a person leaving your site faster than significant mistakes in your content.

You are an expert in your retail business; at least, that is what the target audience will assume. A non-expert will have errors on their website and a non-user-friendly experience, at least that is the assumption, mainly when a user sees errors.

While writing naturally, you want to avoid language that may not fit your target consumer. A good rule is to write at a 7th to 8th-grade level. According to literacy studies, the average American reads and writes at a 7th to 8th-grade level, with only 15% of the population reading at full literacy or what you would consider a doctorate level.

**Hire a Writer**

If you know your strength is not in writing, hire a writer. There are plenty of writers out there willing to create website content. Finding one is easy, as long as you know how to search. Be specific that you want to see written samples, and the writer needs to be a native English speaker. Also, be willing to pay a livable wage to ensure the quality of the content.

If you are unsure if you have the budget, think of the time it would take you to create quality content. Is it worth $10 per every 1,000 words to get quality content when you might spend 5 hours on one page of content?

If there are grammar or spelling mistakes, note how many there are before getting upset at your writer. You had probably made mistakes, even when you tried not to in your business. It can happen. An untalented writer is an error in every sentence or two sentences, but one mistake in 10,000 words of content is not. A recent book often on the New York Bestseller list had "jury-rigged" instead of "jerry-rigged," when talking about setting up a place to work. It is published for thousands to read, yet it has a mistake. The writer, editor, or editing software may have been responsible for the error.

**1,000 to 1,250 Words of Content**

Google creators have changed their views on the number of content website pages should have. It used to be 300 words, which was suitable for website pages. Now, 1,000 to 1,250 words are more appropriate. However, do not be married to only one length.

First and foremost, the content needs to be natural, without forcing the subject or adding in fluff. You wouldn't read this book if it kept repeating things over and over to make the word count correct? No, of course, you wouldn't; thus, your website content should be an appropriate length that details the subject, without repetition or fluffy words.

Some pages will require less content. You don't need 1,000 words to tell someone how to contact you, but you do need around 1,000 words to discuss your experience, your business, and other essential employees. You want to outline your return policy, refund policy, and additional specific retail information with as much detail as possible.

## Evergreen Content not a Must

In previous years, evergreen content was a must. Website content creators wanted the content to last for years without being rewritten. Now, this has changed. The way to keep your website relevant is to have frequently updated content.

Marketing News and Codeable agree that you need to write and write to ensure you have something for the user. Original content is imperative, whether you upload written, video, or image-based content.

The newer your content, the more frequently Google bots will search your site and refresh the index and page ranking. If there is nothing new to add to your main website pages, then yes, by all means, go with evergreen content so that minor, quick updates can be made.

Imagine if your users come to your site once a week for two months, but you never had anything new. This user will determine that you are not updating your site, that all the information has been gleaned from it, and they are no longer interested.

# Chapter 5 - Google Quality Score: What it Means and How to Make It Higher

One thing to remember about Google is that it is all about the numbers and the rankings. Every aspect of your campaign will be measured and assigned a place within Google's different algorithms. Every detail is relevant when you are setting up your ad on Google because Google is constantly monitoring and calculating the performance of your data and because you need to be careful that changing algorithms won't mess with your ads.

No one wants to spend more on their advertisement than they have to, and the Google Quality Score will help you to keep the costs of your campaign as low as possible. If you make ads that don't match up well, or do keyword stuffing or do other things that will anger your customers and make for a lousy advertisement using AdWords, then your score is going to be lower, and you will have to pay more for the keywords that you want to use.

However, if you make sure that you write high-quality ads for your campaigns, follow the rules, pick out good keywords, and follow the other rules that come with Google AdWords, you will find that you will get a higher score. And this results in better bid prices, which bring you the visibility you want, without the high costs.

Let's take a look at what the Google Quality Score is all about and how a marketer will use this number to help effectively grow their audience without spending a ton of extra money.

## What Is the Google Quality Score?

Each ad on AdWords will have a quality score from Google. The keywords used in your ad will also receive this score. Google has an algorithm to determine if an ad is doing well or not, and some of the different aspects that will help you to get a higher score would include:

1. The CTR or click-through rate. This value is the percentage of people who click on your ad when they see it.

2. The relevance of the keywords to the ad. It measures how well the keyword will match the text you have in the ad.

3. The quality of the landing page. It evaluates how the page is written and optimized, the keyword, and the ad relevance.

4. The quality and relevance of ad text to the keywords and the landing page.

5. The average account performance with AdWords over a given period.

So, why should you work on this quality score? A higher score can help lower the amount you pay in bid rates, and it can ensure that the ad will rank higher. This means that you can get more out of your budget and get more customers to your page.

**Ways That You Can Improve the Google Quality Score**

The good news is that there are steps that you can take to improve the Google Quality Score that you have. Some of the measures that you can take to maximize your ad performance and get the highest Google Quality Score possible include:

- Keyword relevance: Make sure that the display URL and the ad copy are relevant to the targeted keywords.
- The landing page's relevance: You should optimize your landing pages to give your visitors a message and experience consistent with your ad.
- Test the different ad text variations to see which type of phrasing seems to get the best click-through rate.
- Build out the negative keyword list. It helps narrow the target

audience and ensures that you don't waste your budget on the wrong people.

To ensure that you get your ads placed in the best spots and for a chance to get better visibility for less spending, you need to make sure that you have a boost to your Google Quality Score. If you follow the tips in the rest of the guidebook, you will naturally have a great Quality Score to help you out.

# GOOGLE ADWORDS

# Chapter 6 -Creating Compelling Ads

What makes up a Google AdWords ad? A basic Google AdWords ad consists of four lines. They include a Headline, a URL, and two description lines. Generally, we find a Call-To-Action (CTA) in the second description line, directing prospects toward a particular action. The first character of each word on every line of an ad, except the URL, must be uppercase. All other characters in the terms are lower case. It is important to note that while an exclamation point can appear in any ad line excluding the URL, only one exclamation can occur in the entire ad. All other punctuation can be used as needed. Vulgar language is unacceptable, and brand names may appear in an ad only if Google receives written permission from the trademark owner. Let's take a closer look at these lines in the order that they appear in the ad.

## Creating a headline

The headline is designed to grab the prospect's attention. It must be eye-catching and different from the competition's ads. One way to accomplish this is to include at least one keyword in the headline, which can be no longer than twenty-five characters (always remember when calculating length that spaces count as characters).

Strategies that should be used in the headline are:

- Always be professional. Be mindful not to offend prospects.
- Try beginning with a question. A question engages the chance.
- Get to the point. Space and time are limited. So, get to the point quickly. A prospect spends seconds comparing ads. Be specific about the offer, including a price and CTA. Avoid engaging irrelevant prospects and wasting clicks.

- Include keywords. Keywords increase the relevancy of the text and are automatically displayed in bold, making them easier to find in the ad. Try to use them wherever possible, including in the URL. Also, the usage of keywords may reduce the cost for better placement on the SERP.

- Extend the Headline. An ad may be displayed in a larger format if it appears in the first two positions of page one, and there is punctuation at the end of the first description line. This pulls the first description line up to extend the headline.

Example: Water Heater Busted? Install & Repair in 24 Hours.Licensed + Insured. Free Quotes!

Use abbreviations or symbols. Tighten up the text to maximize the information.

## Creating a destination URL

The Destination URL, commonly referred to as the URL, is the address for the location that appears after the prospect clicks on the ad. The destination should be a landing page and not the homepage to expedite lead generation. The URL can be up to thirty-five characters and should contain no spaces. All characters in the URL should be lowercase. As with the headline, it is recommended to use a keyword that continues to match the prospect's search. If more than one keyword is used in the URL, they can be separated with an underscore or hyphen between the words.

**TIP:** Avoiding the home page. The chance of converting a prospect from a home page is slim because it offers too many options. The URL should go to a landing page.

## Creating description lines

The First Description line should indicate the benefits and/or features of the product/service. It is recommended to include a time frame/limitation to encourage a sense of urgency (if possible). The first description line can be up to thirty-five characters, including spaces.

## Description line 1

Strategies to be used in the description line one:

- Always promote the benefits to get prospects to click.
- Use Numbers because they are easy to read. They can represent the value of an offer (20% Discount), validate the vendor's success (2.5 million Sold), or create a sense of urgency like, offer ends 6/11/15.

## Description line 2

The Second Description line indicates the benefits and/or features of the product/services and should include a Call-to-Action. Furthermore, the CTA invites the prospect to click on the ad to receive free quotes. This CTA further helps differentiate this service from the competition and further engages the prospect.

Strategies for the second description line include:

- An exclamation mark. Only one exclamation mark is permitted per ad. Use it to bring attention and/or a sense of urgency to a CTA. Exclamation marks cannot be used in the headline, only once in either description line one or description line two.
- Abbreviations or symbols. Tighten up the text to maximize the information.
- Include an offer. An offer stimulates interest.
- A Call-to-Action (CTA). Get the prospect to take the next step by providing an action such as an opportunity to sign up, purchase, or

get information. Be sure to set a time limit and include an exclamation mark to get an immediate click! Often used CTA's include:

Buy Now!

Read the White Paper!

Learn More!

Register Now!

Contact Sales!

Get a Free Trial!

Read More!

Limited Time Offer!

**Strategies for creating engaging ads**

A strategy that consistently produces good results is often a best practice. Here is a list of best practice strategies to create an ad that effectively engages prospects and maximizes clicks.

- **Include keywords.** Keywords increase the relevancy of the text and are automatically displayed in bold, making them easier to find in the ad. Try to use them whenever possible, including the URL. Also, the usage of keywords may reduce the cost for better placement on the SERP. (See on Quality Score.)

- **Use an exclamation mark.** Only one exclamation mark per ad is permitted. Use it to bring attention and/or a sense of urgency to a CTA or perhaps one description line.
- **Promote benefits.** Always promote the benefits to get prospects to click.
- **Include a value proposition.** A value proposition, such as Free Shipping or 20% Discount, provides an extra bonus and makes the ad stand out.
- **Include numbers.** Numbers are easy to read. They can represent the value of an offer (20% Discount), validate the success of the vendor (2.5 million Sold), or create a sense of urgency (offer ends on 6/11/15).
- **Avoid the home page.** The chance of converting a prospect from a home page is slim because it provides too many options. The URL should go to a landing page.
- **Use Trademarks.** One trademark is permitted per ad. It conveys a sense of trust and confidence. Be sure to get written permission as needed.

  To obtain written permission for Trademarks – 3rd party Google Authorization Request, use the following URLs.

  https://services.google.com/inquiry/aw_tmauth?

- **Use the word "you".** Address the ad directly to the prospect.
- **Use abbreviations or symbols.** Tighten up the text to maximize the information.
- **Site Links - Ad Extensions.** The more space an ad occupies, the

better the chance a prospect will click on it. The Site Links feature accepts up to six additional links.

- **Optimizing an ad.** For optimizing an ad, include a minimum of two ads in every ad group to see which performs better. The AdWords optimization feature allows the more popular ad to place higher on the SERP. Change one thing on the lower placing ad and rerun the campaign. If top performance is not achieved, continue changing one item at a time until the desired performance is reached.

**Key Takeaways**

For a successful Google AdWords campaign, the marketer must create an engaging ad.

A basic Google AdWords ad consists of four lines. They are:

- **The headline** is designed to grab the prospect's attention.
- **The Destination URL**, commonly referred to as the URL, is the address for the location that appears after the prospect clicks on the ad.
- **The First Description line** should indicate the benefits and/or features of the product/service.
- **The Second Description line** indicates the benefits and/or features of the product/services and should include a Call-to-Action.

**Test Your Knowledge**

1. A Google AdWords ad consists of all except:

a. Headline
b. Descriptive line
c. Display URL
d. Landing Page

2. An exclamation mark can be used as many times as needed in an AdWords ad.

a. True
b. False

3. The best strategy for a Google AdWords ad is never to use a CTA because it is very pushy to the prospect, and ads should be informative and too offensive.

a. True
b. False

4. Which of the following components can be up to 25 characters, including spaces?

a. Display URL

b. First Description line

c. Second Description line

d. Headline

**Test Your Knowledge** *Answers*

1. A Google AdWords ad consists of all except:

a. Landing Page

2. An exclamation mark can be used as many times as needed in an AdWords ad.

b. False

3. The best strategy for a Google AdWords ad is to never use a call-to-action because it is very pushy to the prospect and ads should be informative and not pushy.

b. False

4. Which of the following components can be up to 25 characters, including spaces?

d. Headline

5. What can the display URL not contain?

a. an exclamation point

# Chapter 7 - Optimizing for Conversions

The reason for tracking all these conversions is to "optimize" the campaign based on the conversion data we acquire. I put that word in quotation marks because it gets thrown around a lot when people talk about their AdWords campaigns. The problem with the term, in my opinion, is that it implies perfection – that somehow the campaign will reach an "optimized" state where it is no longer able to be improved. This isn't true. There is always room for improvement.

Nonetheless, I will use the word anyway. Just keep in mind that I am talking about a process rather than an elusive result.

Conversion optimization is probably the most critical and complex process to undertake in an AdWords account. Once everything else is in order, it's the primary thing that will determine the long-term success of a campaign. It's highly technical, and it's the main reason clients pay my students and me thousands of dollars a month to manage their AdWords accounts.

I'll do my best to break down the basics of conversion optimization right now.

Essentially, we're looking to maximize traffic from the components of the account that are generating a profit and decrease or eliminate traffic from elements that are not generating profit.

Depending on the conversion tracking you have in place, and how much you know about your conversions (profit margin, value per lead, etc.), it can be very easy or extremely tricky to determine profitability.

Whether or not you know your exact numbers, you need to value your conversions and use that value when optimizing your campaigns. This value will be our target cost per conversion. Sometimes it makes sense to start with a target conversion cost that is at or above break-even, as this will allow you to gather more data more quickly to create a more profitable campaign eventually. You can constantly adjust target conversion cost later.

When optimizing for conversions, there are several factors to consider.

**Campaign Conversion Data**

If our target cost per conversion is $10, and we've already spent $500 on the campaign with only two conversions, then we've got a lot of work to do. In that example, we can do nothing to start optimizing for conversions. If the campaign is already set up according to the strategies outlined in this book and the keywords in the search term report look good, a more realistic place to start would be with the website or the product itself. Maybe the website needs a serious overhaul. Or perhaps the product isn't right for AdWords.

If, instead, we've spent $500, and we've received 40 conversions, we are in a much better place to start optimizing the campaign for conversions. The cost per conversion is $12.50, so it should be easy to bring this down to $10.00 or less.

One approach might be to simply decrease all bids in the campaign. This operation will lower the cost per click, which will translate to a lower cost per conversion (assuming the conversion rate stays the same).

This can be a quick fix, but we may also be sacrificing some good traffic by bidding less per click. Whether or not we are spending our entire budget every day, we might even end up with fewer conversions (and less profit) overall.

So rather than decrease all of our bids, a winning conversion optimization strategy will use other data points within the account.

**Ad Group Conversion Data**

Take a look at the cost per conversion for each of your ad groups. Is one ad group responsible for the bulk of your conversions? This is often the case, and there's nothing necessarily wrong with this. By looking at the ad groups you are spending most of your budget on, you can start to look for differences.

Perhaps one ad group has a cost per conversion of $20, and another has a cost per conversion of $8. If there are at least a few conversions in each ad group, you can start to make adjustments. In this case, we would decrease the bid for the ad group with the $20 conversions and increase the bid for the ad group with the $8 conversions.

I said "at least a few conversions" because it is essential to make sure there is enough data to justify these decisions. If you have an ad group that has spent $5 and received one conversion, this doesn't mean that the ad group will have an average cost per conversion of $5. It means there isn't enough data yet to make that decision, so that we would leave things alone. We need at least a few conversions to start figuring out an average.

However, suppose we've spent 2x or 3x our target cost per conversion, and we've received zero conversions. In that case, we can start decreasing those bids and eventually removing those ad groups entirely. We don't want to make rash decisions (the next conversion could be right around the corner), but if we're not getting any conversions from something, we don't want to keep spending money on it forever either. It's a fine line.

I usually start to decrease bids when campaign components are 2x my target cost per conversion, and I begin to consider removing components once I reach 3x-4x my target with zero conversions. You might change things sooner or later depending on how much you can afford to invest in getting things working. This goes for ad groups bids and for all the other components I will be discussing in this chapter.

## Keyword Conversion Data

Like with your ad groups, you may find that specific keywords are getting most of your traffic and conversions. It takes longer for the data to accumulate (compared to ad group data) since it is split across many keywords. Still, eventually, you will find specific keywords are performing better or worse than others.

When you find keywords with a good amount of traffic and a high or low cost per conversion, you should start to adjust the bids for those keywords.

Again, if a keyword has a high cost per conversion, you should decrease your bid for that keyword. If a keyword has a low cost per conversion, you should increase your bid for that keyword.

This may sound relatively simple so far – decreasing and increasing bids – but here's where it starts to get more complex: After we start making these changes, other things are going to change. AdWords traffic and customer behavior are not static, but it is fluid. The conversions rates will not stay the same, and there are other changes we will make to the campaign that will affect overall performance.

Conversion optimization isn't a one-time thing. It's a process. (Have I made this clear yet?)

## Other Conversion Data

Inside your AdWords account, you will find results and numbers to help you optimize for conversions.

I'll say again: In all cases, we are looking to maximize traffic from the components of the account generating a profit and decrease or eliminate traffic from elements that are not generating profit.

Here are some of the other data points to evaluate and consider when making these adjustments:

- Search partner network (you can't increase or decrease bids for this traffic, but you can turn it off if it isn't generating any conversions)
- Locations (countries, states, cities, zip codes, neighborhoods, etc.)
- Schedule (times of day and days of the week)
- Devices (mobile, desktop, and tablet)
- Audiences (remarketing and in-market)
- Demographics (age, gender, income – Note: Google's household income targeting is not very good)

## Compounding Bid Adjustments:

As you can see, there are a lot of places in AdWords where we can adjust the bids. There are a lot of settings that can be changed that will affect other settings, and they often compound on each other. Let's say, for example, you've applied the following bid adjustments to a campaign:

Mobile +15%

Canada +15%

Tuesday +15%

You may have data that justify each of these changes. But if someone on a mobile device, in Canada, on a Tuesday, searches for your ad, your bid adjustment for that person is +45% (it's not exactly 45%, the formula works out a little different than that, but to simplify it we can just say 45%). Does your data justify a change that big? Probably not.

So be mindful of those possibilities. If your campaign shows significant differences in performance among these options, consider splitting them up into separate campaigns. Perhaps you would end up with campaigns that look like this:

Canada + Mobile

Canada + Desktop/Tablet

USA + Mobile

USA + Desktop/Tablet

So now, instead of one campaign, we have four. We can then adjust the bids more precisely in each campaign. This isn't always necessary, but it can certainly be helpful if you need to avoid the compounding effects of too many bid adjustments.

**Search Term Conversions**

We analyze the search term report the same way we study the keyword data. Any search terms that are getting conversions should be added to the campaign as exact match keywords. We can then bid on them using the search term report data as our starting point.

In general, when you're looking through your search term report, you should be adding every search term you see as an exact match keyword or a negative keyword. You need to decide whether or not you want to target every keyword. If it's a keyword you wish to, don't rely on a broad match or a phrase match keyword to capture it. Add it as an exact match keyword, so you have more control over the bid in the future.

**Ads: Stand Up, Shout, & Get Noticed (By The Right People)**

A well-crafted, engaging ad will bring customers to your website. For the most part, you want ads that accomplish this goal.

But there's a catch: A higher click-through rate usually equals a lower conversion rate.

Imagine analyzing data from two ads that were running in the same ad group during the same period:

Notice that the first ad has a significantly higher CTR and a lower conversion rate. Both ads generated the same number of conversions, but the first ad cost us TWICE as much as the second.

I'll admit that this is an extreme example. But when you test enough ads, you'll notice that this correlation almost always exists.

So what's going on here?

Both ads attract the same number of buyers to click on them, but the ad with the higher CTR attracts a lot more non-buyers. This could be because the ad is written too well to trigger the user's curiosity, but your actual product or service is not attractive to them. There may also be a discontinuity between your ad and landing page causing most people to leave. Only the hardcore customers, who are desperately in need of what you're selling, stick around long enough to make a purchase.

When split-testing ads, you should always split tests based on cost per conversion. The ad with the lowest cost per conversion will be the winner.

An exception to this will be if your cost per conversion is already so low that you can afford to pay more if it means you will generate more overall conversions. In this case, your cost per conversion may be higher, but your net profits will be higher as well.

Because of all this, it almost sounds like writing killer ads isn't that important since you may pay the price if your ads are too good. However, getting customers to come to your website is still the number one goal of an AdWords ad. If people aren't converting once they get there, you need to look at the landing page experience or the types of people and keywords you are targeting in your campaign.

With this in mind, I'll discuss what it takes to write killer ads.

# Chapter 8 - Tips on Improving your Content Marketing Strategy

Content marketing is a difficult skill to master; there is so much new content arriving online every day that your content can easily be swallowed up and vanish into the murky world of the internet, to vanish forever.

As well as having to compete with other content, you must also be aware of the increasing demand that consumers place on instant results. If your content is graphic-heavy, it may take too long to load, and your potential customer has moved on to something else. The same is also true if your website takes too long to load.

The best way to avoid this issue is to create content that stimulates your readers and stays with them, even after reading. This can be harder to reach than you imagine! The following tips should help you to shape your content to ensure it rises above the other postings on the web.

**Display**

It is essential to ensure your content displays well over a wide range of media as with your marketing strategy. The best approach to this is to use a relatively new technique, known as responsive design. This ensures your content is displayed well on a desktop computer, laptop, tablet, mobile phone, or other devices.

Ensuring your content is well displayed and loads quickly, even on a mobile phone, effectively increase sales. This is also becoming increasingly important for your ranking in the search engines as they are now taking mobile usage into account when calculating the rankings. This is a direct response to statistics that now show that forty percent of people access the internet via their handheld devices.

## Customer Needs

Every client has various desires and needs and may have taken a different route to your site and your content. It is necessary to differentiate between where they are in the process and what their needs are likely to be to provide the best possible experience and increase the effectiveness of your content marketing. The first part is if this is achieved by using cookies; this will establish whether they have visited your site before. New arrivals may wish to see all the options and learn about your business, whereas returning customers may prefer to be directed straight back to the last product they purchased and shown similar items.

The experience will be faster and better, ensuring your customer absorbs the necessary content and returns again and again.

## Navigation

Your website must be easy to navigate with a layout conducive to the eye and easy to use. Most people read from left to right and from top to bottom. This means that the navigation tabs should be at the top of the page in a left to the right style.

The easier it is to find what they are looking for, the more likely they will purchase something from your site.

This ease of navigation should be applied to every content article you write; a link from your article to your website should take your visitor directly to the page they want; this will increase the efficacy of your content and the likelihood of a sale.

## The Content

One of the most challenging contents to write is the product description; there is so much you can say about some products, which the manufacturer often summarizes. Many businesses use the manufacturer's product description on their site; copying and pasting are quicker and easier than creating new content.

However, the search engines respond best to new content; it is better to create a new description for each product and create just a few each day. The search engines will rate you higher because you are posting original content and posting regularly!

There is a secondary reason for creating these unique descriptions and completing additional articles regularly. The search engines operate what is known as 'crawlers'; these pieces of software trawl the web and look for new material. Sites that have fresh material are deemed more active relevant and will feature higher in the search engine rankings.

The more content you post, the more often the crawler will recognize your site, and your ranking will be better!

## Product Ideas

A very effective way of posting additional content and improving your customer relations is to add a short spiel to each sale. These must be relevant to the product. For example, if you sell a hammer, you could suggest a way of keeping the hammer safe or how to use it; you could even provide tips on keeping your thumb out of the way when using it!

Every piece of information will endear your customer to you, particularly if you can add some humor to it. The best details can be added to your social media account and linked to your website to encourage additional followers.

An additional content marketing strategy that can produce excellent results is to provide a section on your website where customers can leave their reviews and feedback. These reviews can be highlighted by using the right software, and they can then actually be picked up by Google! In turn, these snippets will be used by Goggle on their search results page and can result in a higher click-through rate. Providing your website has been well designed, and the tips in this book have been applied, you should be able to convert some of these into additional sales.

**Add a Seal**

Anyone can write content, although it is relatively apparent when written by someone who understands the subject. It is a good idea to become accredited by a relevant organization to increase your trustworthiness. This can be the approval by an organization such as the better business bureau or an endorsement from a manufacturer.

**Budget and Review**

The first rule of any business expenditure is to budget; decide what you can afford to invest in content marketing and stick to the budget. There is no point in attracting lots of potential customers if you are not making any money! If you write your content yourself, it may seem as though creating it is free; but this is never the case. When you spend time writing content, you could be doing other work, whether this is producing your product, reducing other overheads, or even coming up with the next big thing! While content is essential to building an online following and creating a customer base, other items need your attention.

Of course, if you pay someone else to write the content for you, there is an undeniable cost. Once the budget is set, you will need to look at where the funds are going and the success of the various content marketing campaigns. If you do not do this, you may discover that your time and effort are being spent in the wrong direction; for example, Facebook is the biggest social platform, so it would seem to make sense to put the majority of your content there. However, your product may be more visually appealing, and you may have much more success from a smaller social site, something like Pinterest, which focuses on images. Choose the proper arena to spend your money in!

## Guidelines

One of the most important parts of your content postings is that they remain consistent. While the actual content is different, the approach and presentation should stay the same. This will assure the reader that they know what they are getting; they will not be bombarded with information they do not need. You may choose to tell a funny story in the first two paragraphs; the story will highlight an issue you will solve in the third paragraph. You could then close with some helpful tips on using this product and a call to action.

Again, there is no right or wrong approach to this, but you do need to develop a strategy that works and is consistent, even if you have a team of writers working for you. Guidelines can be essential if you have a team of writers; it will give them the correct information to do the job correctly. Your guidelines should include the tone, the feel, and the type of content.

An essential extra part of creating guidelines is the creation of a posting schedule. Customers do not wish to constantly check back to see if you have any new content. Instead, create a program if content will be created and posted. Once you have established your routine, you will simply need to create quality content that answers a need; even if they did not know they had the need! Your customers will learn when your new content is published and return at the right time to digest it.

## Goals

The ultimate goal is probably to be successful and make a profit in your chosen endeavor. However, this is only possible if you set yourself goals. Break down your main goal into smaller, achievable goals. Then, break these down into even smaller goals. Ideally, you want to have a mini target to achieve each day; reaching the daily target will automatically take care of the larger target.

Without establishing goals and working towards them, you will be unable to create a successful online content marketing strategy. Setting them does not mean you cannot change them as your understanding and ambitions change.

## Think Outside the Box

There are many different ways to produce content; the classic article or newsletter is a good tool and something that can be used very effectively to get a specific point across. However, much of your content marketing efforts can be focused on alternative options; video and pictures are becoming increasingly popular, and there are other ways of attracting the attention of those who are already in line.

Allowing yourself time to think will provide you with an opportunity to create unique content which breaks the mold; this can be the key to building a large following very quickly.

## Free Content

You may shudder at the thought of giving your content away, especially if you have paid someone to write it! However, creating content for free will encourage people to read it and make a following that can be turned into sales in the future. All content should have your contact details and a link to your subscriber list, even if these items are at the bottom of the page.

Giving away quality content will also convince people that you are genuine, know your subject, and are trustworthy. They will be much more likely to spend money with you in the future when they need information which is not free!

Online content marketing is an essential part of the business if you wish to succeed.

Online content marketing is an essential part of the business if you wish to succeed. The number of people using social media and the internet to find answers is overgrowing; this means that your potential customer base is also growing rapidly, and you need to jump out at them and show them how good your product is.

It is important to remember that your approach must be different depending on dealing with individuals or other businesses. An individual online will be happy to connect to you emotionally, which is often achieved by telling personal stories. These stories should trigger feelings in the reader as they believe it could happen to anyone. However, businesses work differently; they are all about the bottom line; feelings are rarely part of the equation. Instead, focus on your product's value to their business and back up your claims with data.

To establish the success of your online content marketing strategy, you will need goals and key performance indicators. You will then be able to mark your success against the performance indicators which are essential to you.

# Chapter 9 - Search Campaigns Ad Group Settings & structure

Each of our main ad groups should be created two times, one as Exact match and one as Broad Match Modified (BMM). These ad groups will contain only Exact match keywords or BMM keywords, respectively.

Creating an Exact match keywords ad group is that if a keyword is good enough for us to bid on, we should use it only as an exact match.

The reason for creating a Broad Match Modified keywords ad group is that we want to use it for "mining" keywords. When we run a Search Query Report (SQR) which we will describe later, we will find search queries by BMM keywords that brought users to our site. If they are good to us (got conversions, clicks, etc.), we will then remove them from the BMM ad group and add them as exact match to an Exact match ad group.

Our ad group names should consist of 3 parts:

1. Main ad group name
2. Actual ad group name
3. Match type

This naming convention will make reviewing and optimization much more manageable.

**EXAMPLES**

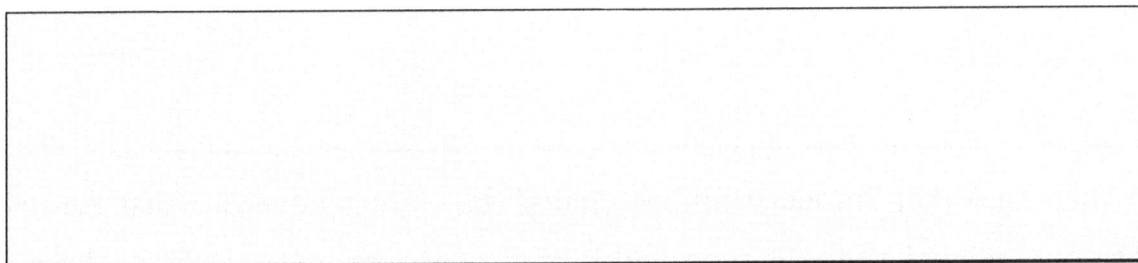

For Dining Chairs under the campaign named Search.Furniture.Chairs, we will create two ad groups named:

Dining Chairs.Dining Chairs.Exact

Dining Chairs.Dining Chairs.Bmm

The exact match ad group will contain the keyword "[dining chair]," and the broad match modified will contain the keyword "+dining +chair".

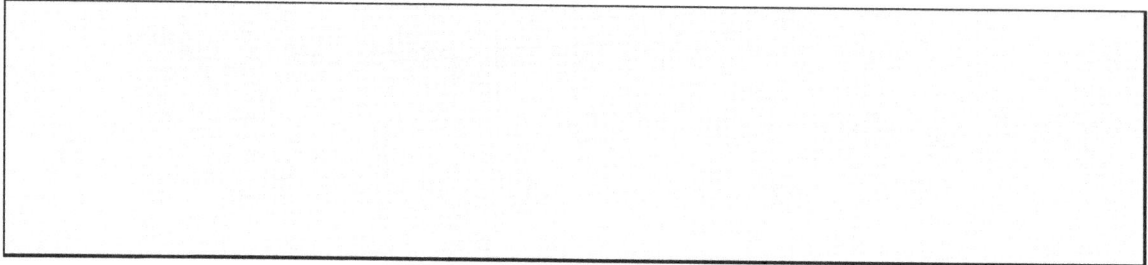

Same, e.g., Round Mirrors under the campaign named Search.Decoration.Mirrors, we will create two ad groups named:

Round Mirrors.Round Mirrors.Exact

Round Mirrors.Round Mirrors.Bmm

Now, the main keyword used in each set of Exact match and Bmm match should be added as a negative keyword from the Bmm group. Thus, we can ensure that when someone searches for, e.g., "Dining Chairs" or "Round Mirrors," only the Exact match ad group will participate in Google's auction. Additionally, when a user searches something similar to our keyword like "wooden dining chairs" or "dining chairs on sale" or "modern dining chairs," we will also be eligible to appear in Google's results since our Dining Chairs.Dining Chairs.Bmm ad group contains the keywords "+dining +chairs."

We might then find that "modern dining chairs" is a great keyword that brings lots of conversions! We will then add it as a negative keyword from the ad group where it initially came from (Dining Chairs.Dining Chairs.Bmm) and create an Exact match ad group which will use the exact match type keyword [modern dining chairs]:

Dining Chairs.Modern Dining Chairs.Exact

As you can see once again, the first part of the name is the main ad group name which tells us that this ad group refers to Dining Chairs, the second part refers to the actual ad group name, and the third part is the match type used.

Also, there is no need to create an additional Bmm ad group for this new ad group since we will still be eligible to show our ads for search terms similar to our new keyword like "cheap modern dining chairs" or "modern dining chairs on sale" by the Dining Chairs.Dining Chairs.Bmm ad group.

As you understand the Main ad group name used as a prefix is very important because:

- You will have a more explicit ad structure. When your ad groups are shorted alphabetically, it will be easy to review and understand your structure.
- By creating a filter and searching for all ad groups containing the name: "Dining Chairs," you can instantly view the total performance of each subcategory. If you use the naming convention as explained in the book across all types of ad groups, you will also be able to view the performance of a subcategory across the whole account and in every kind of campaign.
- It will help us later with our optimizations as this will allow us to perform optimizations at a specific subcategories level.

**Quick Note:** Don't panic about the seemingly huge amount of work needed to structure your ad groups.

**Branding campaign**

We will create one Bmm match and one Exact match ad group on the branding campaign referring to our company. So, we will create a

YourCompany.Exact and YourCompany.Bmm ad groups. The initial Exact match ad group will be used when a user searches for our company on Google. The Bmm match will be used once again for mining keyword ideas when a user searches for our company along with something else, e.g., "examplecompany office desks ."Same as before, if we find search queries that bring conversions, clicks, etc., we would create new ad groups as Exact match only. There is no need to add a prefix here since all ad groups practically point to our brand.

## Competition campaign

At a minimum, create an exact match ad group for each of your competitors. If you want to expand your Competition Campaign even further, add Bmm ad groups and scale your campaign when necessary. For prefix, use the name of your competitor.

## Creating an Ad Group

When you create a new ad group, you will be sent to this screen:

Ad group name

Default bid ⑦

$ 0.10

+keyword
"keyword"
[keyword]

Match types help control which searches can trigger your ads

keyword = Broad match   "keyword" = Phrase match   [keyword] = Exact match   Learn more

Name your ad groups as described and set a default bid of, e.g., $0.10.

We will make all of our optimizations on search campaigns at the keywords level, so if you create an ad group for a search campaign, don't pay attention to the Default bid at the ad group. Once we add bids on keywords, the ad group bids will be ignored.

You can skip the step of adding keywords; we can add them later. Click SAVE AND CONTINUE.

## RLSA: Add Converters & Non-Converters lists to all search campaigns

On all of our Search campaigns, it is a very good practice to bid more for users who have visited our site but did not convert and users who visited our site and converted. The first audience is already familiar with our business so let's try to bring them back to our store! Furthermore, Converters are not just past visitors, they have made a purchase from our company, and it is much easier for them to purchase again. We will need to bid even more for this audience. So, let's create a Converters and a Non-Converters list.

**Create Converters list**

Probably you will have already linked AdWords with Analytics. Analytics has the option to create Audiences lists that will automatically be available to use in AdWords.

For creating a Converters list on Google Analytics:

a. On the bottom left of the Analytics interface, click on Admin

b. Under Property, click on Audience Definitions

c. Click Audiences

d. Click +NEW AUDIENCE

e. Click Import Segment

f. Click on Converters

g. Change the Membership duration to 100 days

h. Name your audience "All Converters 100"

i. Click on Next step

j. Click on +Add Destinations

k. Add the list to your AdWords & Analytics account

l. Click Publish.

**Create Non-Converters list**

a. On the bottom left of the Analytics interface, click on Admin

b. Under Property, click on Audience Definitions

c. Click Audiences

d. Click +NEW AUDIENCE

e. Click Import Segment as we did previously

f. Now click on Non-Converters

g. Click on the pencil icon

h. Click Behavior

i. Change Session Duration to be greater than 2 seconds. This way, we can be sure that we will add users to our list who showed interest in our content and didn't bounce. This simple rule will reduce our Bounce rate a lot.

j. Click Apply

k. Change the Membership duration to 100 days

l. Name your audience "Non-Converters 100"

m. Click on Next step

n. Click on +Add Destinations

o. Add the list to your AdWords & Analytics account

p. Click Publish

Now let's see if everything is set up well. Go to the AdWords interface, click on the wrench icon on the top right of the screen, and under Shared Library, click on Audience manager. You should see your newly created lists there.

**Add Converters & Non-Converters lists to your Ad Groups**

We will now add these two lists to each of our ad groups. Go into each ad group of your search campaigns and do the following:

a. Click on Audiences

b. Click on +AUDIENCES

c. Leave the Observation option checked

d. Click Website visitors

e. Choose your two newly created lists

f. Click Save

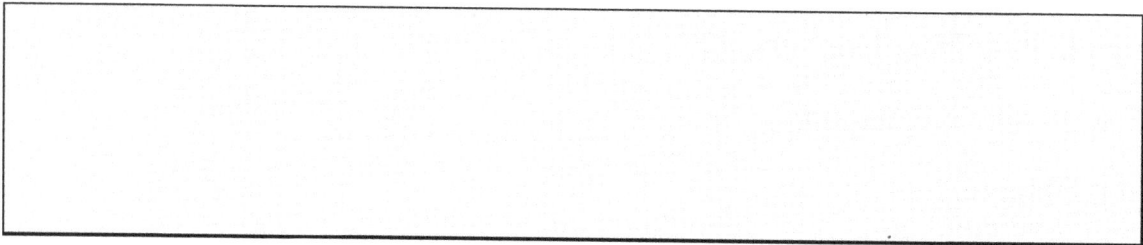

Your lists have been added. Now let's make some bid adjustments. You will see the audiences associated with your ad group on the audience tab. Find the column named Bid adj. Click on the "-" symbol for each audience and make the following adjustments:

Non-Converters 100: Increase by 10%

Converters 100: Increase by 30%

Thus, when a past visitor who didn't convert or a past visitor who converted searches something on Google and his search query is relevant to our ads, we will participate in the auction with increased bids since this user is more valuable to us.

**Quick note:** Be sure to check that you haven't set any goals or conversions on anything different than sales. If you have created a goal for, e.g., a page visit or a conversion action for, e.g., filling up a form, these actions will count as conversions sales which we don't want. If that's the case, you will need to define your audience better.

The following question might have popped up to some of you. If a user visits our site, browse it for 3 seconds, and leaves without a purchase, he is added to our Non-Converters list. What if he comes again and purchases something? Wouldn't he be added to the Converters list as well? What happens in this case since he will belong to two different lists? The answer is that the higher bid always wins, so even if he belongs to two lists, the higher bid (Converters) will be used.

**Dynamic Search Ads (DSA) Ad group structure**

For our DSA campaign, we will create just one ad group to target the whole site. We can create multiple ad groups for different sections of our site for bigger accounts. So, visit your DSA campaign named Search.Dynamic and:

a. Click on +CREATE AD GROUP

b. Be sure that Ad group type is set to Dynamic

c. Name your ad group "All webpages"

d. On the bottom, click on All web pages

e. Click All web pages once again

f. Click SAVE AND CONTINUE

Once again, add the Converters and Non-Converters lists as we did previously using the same bid adjustments.

At this point, be sure to add as many negative keywords as possible before launching your campaign. Upon the first days of launching your DSA campaign, be sure to add negative keywords daily.

**Prospecting campaign (Prsp) Ad Group Settings**

This type of campaign will be used for bringing new visitors to our site. While we could create various prospecting campaigns, we will use just one since it will work fine for most businesses.

**Prospecting campaign ad group structure**

On the prospecting campaign named Prsp, each ad group can refer to any level of the categories of your site you want. So, we could create ad groups for the category Dining Chairs, the category Chairs or the category Furniture, or even all of them. So, map the site categories you would like to run ads (if not all) and go on and create the corresponding ad groups.

For our display campaigns, our ad groups should use the identical same naming convention we used for naming our search campaigns without using the term "Search" in the beginning.

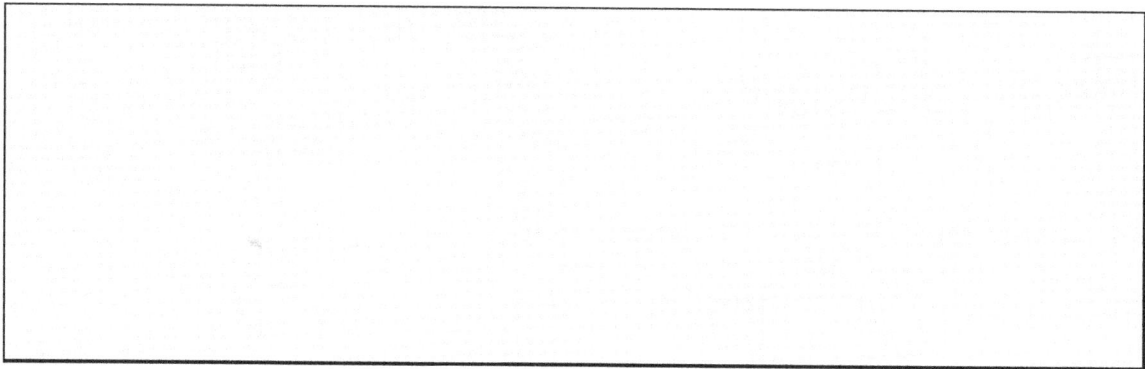

Below are some examples of ad group names we would use:

Furniture.Chairs.Dining Chairs

Furniture.Benches

Decoration.Mirrors.Wall Mirrors

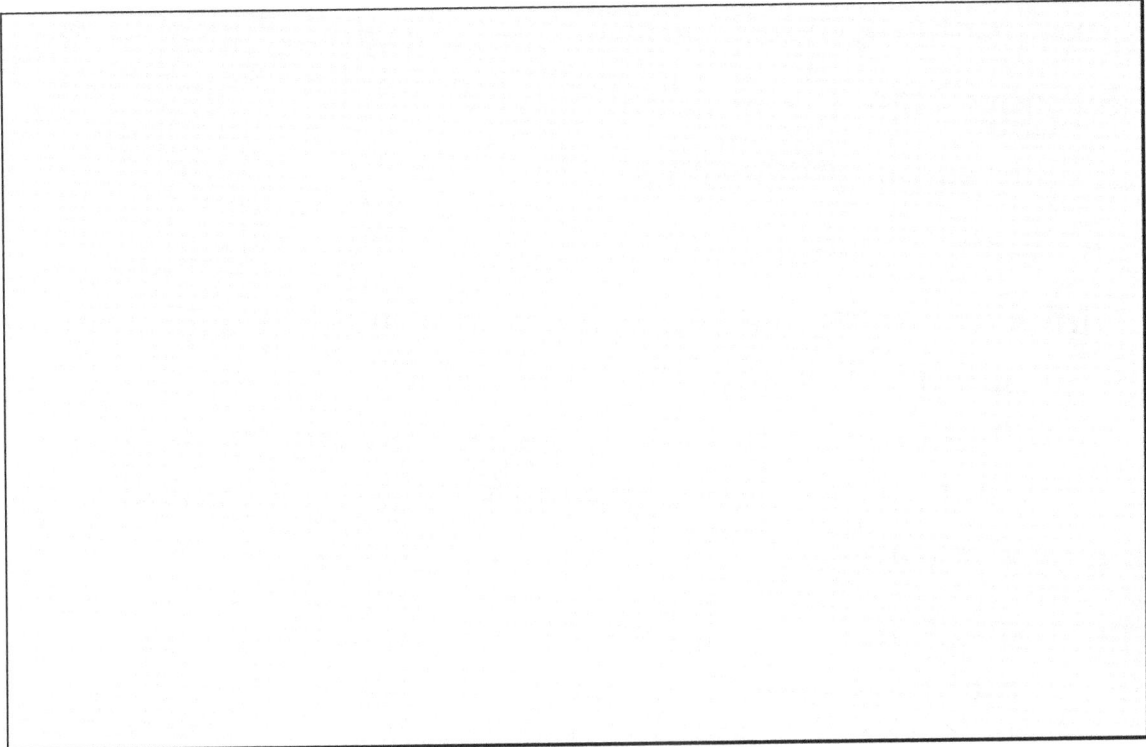

Furthermore, each ad group should be created twice; we will create one ad group running contextual ads and another based on interests (topics) and demographics. Let's give an example of how this would change our naming convention.

Furniture.Chairs.Dining Chairs.contextual

Furniture.Chairs.Dining Chairs.interests

Furniture.Benches.contextual

Furniture.Benches.interests

Decoration.Mirrors.Wall Mirrors.contextual

Decoration.Mirrors.Wall Mirrors.interests

## Contextual ad group settings

With contextual ads, your ads are eligible to be shown when a web page contains one or more keywords you have predefined.

Access each one of your contextual ad groups and do the following:

a. Click on Keywords

b. Click on the button +KEYWORDS

c. Add all relevant keywords of your ad group, one keyword per line.

It is a good idea to use the keywords included in the ad groups of the corresponding search campaign. Don't be bothered about match types; all keywords will be treated as Broad Match. Since keywords will be treated as broad match, it is very important to visit the NEGATIVE KEYWORDS tab and add negative keywords.

Before you click save, be sure to click on Content: Only show ads on web pages, apps, and videos related to these keywords under the Keyword setting. If you want to have an increased reach, you can leave the first option as is, but this will impact performance.

Now, if you want your prospecting ads to appear in some predefined placements on the web, then go to the Placements tab. Add all websites, YouTube channels, etc., you believe are relevant to your business and content.

If you want to target only these placements with content related to the keywords, you will choose Targeting (recommended).

If you want your ads to appear on every related to your keywords webpage AND on your placements (if they have content related to your keywords), choose the "Observation" method. If I want to use placements along with keywords, this is the method I usually use.

If you want to focus on some specific sites but have your ads shown on other web pages, we will have to make some bid adjustments. On the placements tab and after you have added your placements, choose the websites you want to focus on, click on edit, and click on Change bid adjustments. An increase of 30% will do the work.

**Interests ad group settings**

Access each one of your interests ad groups, click on Topics, and then click on the button +TOPICS:

Add all related to your business user interests. Leave the Targeting (recommended) option as is.

Now visit the Demographics tab: Enable/Disable demographics according to your needs. I rarely make any changes here. Don't make any assumptions upfront. You can optimize later on when you have enough data. A rare case scenario where I would make adjustments upfront is when our business is gender-specific, e.g., women's shoe store, men's clothing, etc. If that's the case, add this demographic option to your contextual ad groups as well, and also be sure to make these adjustments in your remarketing campaign.

# Chapter 10 - Facebook and paid advertising

## AdWords vs. Facebook

This is a question that people that are not experienced marketers often ask. The answer is always "it depends." We need to understand the goals we want to achieve with our advertising campaign. It is usually fundamental to combine both strategies. It all depends on the type of question, whether latent or conscious (or both). If the goal is to make branding and then stimulate users who do not know us and may be interested (latent demand), then the best choice is Facebook Ads which will allow you, as we will see later, to reach potential customers. You can do this with various types of targeted campaigns and get leads.

Similarly, you can also use ads on the Google Display Network to reach potential customers by submitting your banners to specific placements. If users are already looking for your product or service, the right approach is to use Google AdWords by creating ads on the Search Network. In this case, the user is already in a much lower part of the funnel, therefore more inclined to purchase as he is looking for your product/service. We will find both types of demand in most cases, and we will have to work on both platforms jointly. The key is to understand where the user is inside our sales funnel and act accordingly; we will never stress it.

Going inside, it will be useful to retarget users who have shown interest in the product or service working with both Facebook Ads and AdWords through ads on the display network.

**Note:** what if we intercept potential customers on Facebook through FB Ads and look for us on Google, but we are not positioned organically (without paying) for that keyword?

Simple, they will click on a competition link. The risk is, therefore, to practically advertise competitors. Understand well then how important it is, in the absence of organic positioning with SEO, that we must also have Google ads on the search network to cover some keywords.

The fact is that Facebook marketing is not so powerful if done alone. It is something that some people see as a disadvantage.

Each Facebook campaign consists of 3 levels, and it starts from the campaign level, which consists of one or more ad groups. As you have just read, you will have to choose a goal for each campaign you create. This is the real distinctive factor at the campaign level.

At the Ad Group level (Ad Set), you will have to choose the target, the available budget, the publication times, the offer, and the placements (placements). Going down the hierarchy, at the level of the announcements, you can set the type of announcement (image, video, carousel, etc.), all the texts, the call to action (action button), and the destination links.

**The Definition of the Goals**

Now that we understand the structure of a Facebook campaign and the parameters to be set for each level, we are ready to launch our first campaign. The first question is, "What is the goal to be achieved?" Do you want to sell a specific product because maybe you have an e-commerce store, want to create awareness or reputation, or do you want to have leads or what?

Often, in a complete web marketing strategy, we will have to create different campaigns for the different phases of the purchasing process. We can then create different ads depending on whether the target user does not know our brand or knows it but does not know our product/service, or for example, knows our product/service and may be interested in a commercial offer.

In the creation phase, Facebook itself will propose different objectives divided into four macro-categories. Let's see them in detail one by one.

## Brand Awareness

When to use it: In large-scale campaigns, there is no particular action that you want to take to the user. This goal will be more attractive to large companies that can afford to launch campaigns for pure branding. However, for smaller companies, almost every other objective will give better and more significant results.

## Reach

When to use it: Similar to the brand awareness goal, the reach objective is functional to reach the maximum number of users the ad will show. With the introduction of the rules, Facebook now allows you to cap the frequency with which the ad is shown to the same user. In this sense, the goal for reach becomes very useful when working with a relatively small audience, and you want everyone to view the ad.

## Traffic

When to use it: When we want to take users to a website, or for example, on a landing page, it is a very interesting goal when promoting content, such as a blog post.

## Leads

When to use it: The lead ads greatly simplify the mobile device signup process. When someone clicks on the ad, a form opens with all personal contact information already pre-filled based on the information they share on Facebook, such as name, surname, phone, and email address. This aspect makes the process fast and within two clicks, one to open the ad and one to send the information.

The only problem with this type of objective is that the email address used to sign up for Facebook several years ago is obsolete and has not been updated for too long. In this case, we would get a useless contact. As a result, it has been seen that better conversion campaigns perform that point to specific external landing pages with data to be filled out.

Another aspect to keep in mind is that lead ads do not allow you to include all the information you want in the offer, like on a landing page. Therefore, for campaigns that require a great deal of cognitive attention from the user, a campaign for conversions will be more successful. That said, in any case, it is always better to do a test between the two approaches and see which performs better because each case and sector can behave differently.

The success of a Facebook campaign depends almost entirely on how we select the right target. Good results are not obtained by trying to guess the interests but only by experimenting and testing and knowing the right tools.

## The pixel of Facebook

Fabio Sutto, a Facebook expert, says it is categorical. The pixel of Facebook should always be installed anyway, even if at the moment we are not interested in campaigning and even if we believe we do not need anything. But why? Because when it is installed (by entering a code on our website), it starts recording data. The pixel will then be able to make us reach users who come into contact with our site, and these users can be used in the future for our listings. It must be installed "regardless" because we may regret not collecting the data when these will help us.

## Spy on competitors' sponsorships

Coming into an advertisement published by our competitors can be a golden opportunity. We can "spy" the target they have chosen for their sponsorship. Just clicking on the 'Why do I view this ad?', the magic is accomplished; we will see exactly what target has set our competitor.

Whether the interests that our competitor has selected works or not, we do not know; however, we can get an idea based on the vanity metrics. And in any case, we now have some tools to test.

## Create a personalized audience

Facebook gives us many options to intercept our potential customers, and we should always start with our customers or our traffic. For example, we can upload a file with our LinkedIn contacts or newsletter subscribers. We can take advantage of the pixel and select who visits specific site pages or generates events (such as sales or add to cart), who spends more time on the site or who visits him more often, or who opens the newsletter.

## Take advantage of other channels, like AdWords

The ads on Facebook certainly do not answer any conscious question. We launch the bait to a potentially interested public and hope that someone will realize that they need our product or service. With ads on AdWords, we intercept the conscious need; the user needs the tires and searches on Google, find our ad, and land on our site.

Well, we can take advantage of the results obtained from AdWords. Such as? Just leave the pixel of Facebook "listening" and create our custom audience based on traffic on the site with the data obtained. At that point, the user who has seen our model X of tires but who has not completed the purchase will see "chased" from our product even within Facebook.

## Use A/B testing

The analysis of the results obtained must always be exploited to our advantage. Facebook gives us the opportunity with A/B testing.

## Facebook Campaigns: Rules to Define the Budget

The risk of wasting money on Facebook campaigns is very high. There are a series of precautions that it is best to undertake to avoid spending our money badly.

Rules to improve CPAs (cost per action) by working on the budget:

- Do not choose too ambitious self-optimization goals. This is especially true for e-commerce, but it is always applicable. It takes several daily conversions high enough for campaigns to learn effectively and improve their performance. We use micro-conversions, i.e., intermediate conversions that are easier to obtain.

- Head different configurations (see advanced planning). When the available budget allows it and "we are allowed to make mistakes," it is good to test different configurations to find the ideal setting.

- Increase the budget progressively. When a campaign proves to be performing, it is normal to want to increase its budget and make it climb; however, the increase must be progressive and for small steps (10% -20%). Or, if there is urgency, better clone the campaign and create a new one with the desired budget. Otherwise, 9/10, there is an increase in CPC and a general decline in performance.
- Do not accept default placements. Always separate positions in groups with the same target until proven otherwise.

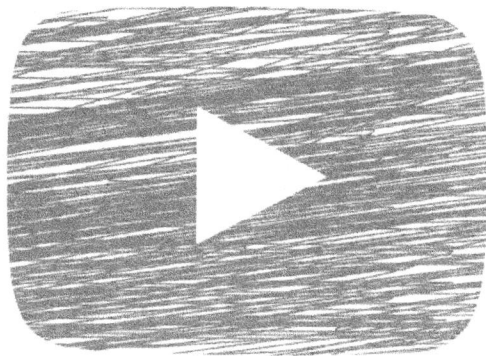

# Chapter 11 - YouTube

I am certain that everyone who has ever used the Internet is aware of how huge YouTube is. In fact, I am also pretty sure that, at some point, we have all wasted an entire lazy day watching funny YouTube videos. But what not everyone knows is that, besides its ability to entertain, this platform has also become a crucial tool for successful marketers from all over the world.

With over 1.8 billion monthly users (who are actually logged in), over 1 billion hours of watched videos per day, and over 400 hours' worth of video being uploaded every minute, YouTube is the 2nd largest search engine.

Whatever category they might fall under, chances are, a huge chunk of your target audience is already on YouTube. Marketing your content on YouTube is a smart move that will help your brand grow by providing more value to your customers.

## Creating Your Business Profile

Before we get right into setting up your business YouTube account and creating your profile, we first need to make sure that you have an active Google account. As you may know, YouTube is owned by Google, and by owning a Gmail account, you can access YouTube logged-in.

But wait before opening YouTube and beginning the profile creation process. Tying up your YouTube profile to your already existing mail may not be such a good idea, especially if we are talking about your business Gmail account. Sharing your access to your YouTube profile with everyone in your company who has access to your business email is not that recommended. For that purpose, it is smart to open a different Gmail account:

1. Go to www.google.com and select the 'Sign In' button found in the upper right corner.

2. Go to 'Create' -> 'Create Account'

3. Fill out the details by entering your name, the name of the email, password, birthday, etc., and click on 'Next Step'.

4. Verify your account by entering your phone number, where a code number will be sent. Type in the code and click 'Continue'. Your new Gmail account is now up and running.

Now that you have a Gmail account, it is time to set up the actual YouTube account for your brand and create its profile.

To get started, simply visit www.youtube.com. If you are logged in with your Gmail, then you are probably already logged in with YouTube. If not, click on the 'Sign In' button in the upper right corner and enter your Gmail and its password. Once you are in, click on the button of your Gmail account in the upper right corner, and select 'My Channel'. You will have the option to create your channel right away, but for your purpose, choose 'Use a Business or Other Name' from the bottom of the page. Now, enter the name of your brand and then click 'Create'. Keep in mind that this can be updated later from your settings menu.

**Channel Icon and Channel Art**

Now that your channel is created, it is time to customize it. Simply select the 'Edit Layout' and let's get started. First, you need to create a channel icon and art. Channel icon and channel art for YouTube are what the profile picture and cover image are for Facebook – they are the first thing that your visitors see and therefore leave the first impression.

Click on the default red picture to add your channel icon. Choose a file from your computer, but keep in mind that this picture will be used on your Grail and Google+ accounts as well; 800 x 800 pixels is recommended here.

Next, click on the 'Add channel art' button found in the center of your channel and upload your preferred image. Here, 2560 x 1440 pixels are recommended.

**Describing Your Brand**

After uploading your pictures, it is time to add some details about your business and customize the 'About' tab. Write a gripping and compelling description that will explain your business briefly and also let people know about the type of videos that will be uploaded on your channel. Make sure to include links to your website and other social media platforms, as well as to include your business email address.

A great option that YouTube provides is the fact that you can customize your channel differently for unsubscribed and subscribed users. The best way to use this option is to add a channel trailer that will lure visitors into hitting the 'subscribed' button.

The channel trailer is a video description of your channel, and it should be short (no longer than 90 seconds; 45 seconds is the best) and appealing. Its main purpose should be to welcome visitors and encourage them to subscribe.

Once you make your channel trailer, it is time to upload it:

1. Make sure that the channel customization is on. You can check this after clicking the settings icon next to 'Subscribe'. Click 'Customize the layout of your channel' and then hit 'Save'.

2. Click on the arrow button found in the upper right corner to upload your trailer. Choose the right file from your PC and click on 'For New Users' once it uploads.

3. Select 'Channel Trailer', choose the file you've uploaded, and hit 'Save'.

Once you get your first 100 subscribers, your channel is more than 30 days old, and you have a channel icon and art uploaded, your YouTube profile will become eligible for a unique and custom URL, which will give it a more professional look.

## Appointing the Roles

Before you start uploading video content and begin your YouTube marketing strategy, you need to indicate how many people on your team will have access to your brand's YouTube channel and their roles.

Once you give them access to the Google account, there are three different role options:

1. Owner: They will have full power, meaning they can add/remove managers, respond/delete comments or reviews, edit information, etc.

2. Manager: Managers can have all of the editing access as the owner without the ability to add or remove other managers.

3. Communications Manager: As the name suggests, the communications manager is mainly in charge of communicating with the audience. They can respond to comments and reviews and do some other editing options. However, they cannot upload new content, view the analytics, or use the video manager. Go to 'Overview' -> 'Add or remove managers' and add individuals to manage your YouTube account.

## Optimizing for SEO

So, you've successfully created your YouTube business channel. Congratulations! But there is so much more to successful marketing than just creating and uploading engaging videos. For people to watch your videos, they will have to find them first. And how can they do so if you haven't optimized the metadata of your videos?

The metadata of your videos is what gives people information about the video such as its title, category, thumbnail, tags, description, subtitles, etc., and providing the right kind of metadata will help your audience discover your video easily, whether on YouTube or Google search.

### Title

When scrolling through the results on YouTube, the first thing that people notice about a video are its title and thumbnail. The title is what hooks the viewer's attention and, therefore, should be well-thought-out. Conduct research to understand what it is that people are looking for. Then, include the relevant keywords and important information in the title, but be careful not to go overboard. If your title has more than sixty characters, it will be shown cut-off in the video result pages on YouTube, and people may not even read the whole thing. Keep it simple, clear, and extremely compelling.

### Description

Just like your title, the description of the video should also contain relevant keywords that will help potential viewers discover your video easily. But as important as the description is, you need to keep in mind that most people do not actually bother to read it. Unless they are interested, that is. Your job is to make them interested. YouTube usually shows only the first 2-3 lines of the description. If viewers want to read the rest of it, they have to click the 'show more' button for the remaining content. Make sure to polish and re-polish the beginning of the description as much as it takes for it to be compelling so that your viewers would want to read the entire content.

If your description contains CTAs or some important links that you want to share with your audience, make sure to include them at the beginning of the description where people will be able to see them even without clicking 'show more'.

Another thing when it comes to writing the description, it is important to always include a transcript of your video. Why? Because your video itself is filled with keywords. By writing a short transcript with these keywords, you will significantly improve your SEO and, eventually, your brand's ranking.

## Tags

Tags are extremely useful because they can associate your brand's videos with other similar videos on YouTube, which only increases their reach and increases your visibility. To that end, make sure your important keywords are tagged. Highlighting the most relevant keywords first is a key part of your brand's SEO optimization, so make sure you choose your words carefully.

## Category

Once your video is uploaded, you will need to choose the category under which it will be shown on YouTube. You can choose the video's category under 'Advanced settings'. You can choose from Film & Animation, Travel & Events, Entertainment, Music, Pets & Animals, Educations, Nonprofits & Activism, People & Blogs, Sports, Autos & Vehicles, How-to & Style, Science & Technology, News & Politics, and Comedy.

Choosing your category carefully is very important as the categories are what group your videos with the relevant ones on YouTube. For instance, if you are selling dog shampoo and list your video under People & Blogs instead of Pets & Animals, you may not reach your target audience.

**Thumbnail**

The thumbnails have a significant impact on the number of views and should be selected carefully. Although YouTube will recommend an option of a few auto-generated thumbnails after uploading, it is highly recommended to skip this option and include a custom thumbnail instead. Choose a shot that will encourage people to click and that represents your video in a good light. YouTube says that 90% of the most successful videos on YouTube actually have custom thumbnails, so you cannot be wrong with this one.

**SRT Files**

Closed captions and subtitles are extremely helpful for viewers, but that is not the only reason why your video should include them. SRT files are also a great way for you to highlight your keywords. Whether you choose to add a timed subtitles file or a transcript of your text, SRT files are a valuable SEO optimization tool that you should definitely take advantage of.

To add SRT files, go to 'Video Manager' -> 'Videos'. There, choose the video to which you want to add the SRT files and select the drop-down arrow on the right. Select 'Subtitles/CC' and choose accordingly.

**End Screens and Cards**

Adding end screens and cards is a valuable option offered by YouTube that can help you encourage your viewers to visit your website, check out your other videos, and even answer poll questions.

Cards are the small notifications that usually appear in the upper right corner of your video. Your card can contain a poll, a link, another video, or can be used to promote another channel on YouTube. You can add up to 5 cards at the same time, but be careful as too many inquiries have the tendency to put off viewers. If you absolutely must add a few cards, make sure to space them out well so that your viewers can take several actions without feeling overwhelmed.

To add a card, go to 'Video Manager' -> 'Cards' -> 'Add Card' and choose whether you want to create a Link, Video or Playlist, Channel, or a Poll card. After creation, simply drag the card to where you want it to appear on the video.

End Screens are those last seconds of the video that encourage the viewers to take further action, such as subscribe to a channel, visit a Facebook page, click the like button, check out another video, etc. You can add 5-20 extra seconds to your videos and ask your viewers to engage with your brand.

To add an end screen, go to 'Video Manager', click on the drop-down arrow, then choose 'End Screens and Annotations'. There, you can choose which elements you want your end screen to include, just keep in mind that it is required to promote another YouTube video or a playlist, so even if you only wanted to encourage viewers to visit your website, you'd have to also encourage people to watch some other video of your brand there.

**Playlists**

You may think that creating playlists is not worth your time, but this feature is a real gem for YouTube marketers. Why? Because it increases your visibility. By creating your playlists, you can combine videos not only from your channels but other YouTube channels as well. And the best part is that these playlists are listed and shown separately in the search results. For instance, if you make a collection of your videos and include some popular ones with similar content, you will help other people who may not have heard about your brand before discovering you.

To create a playlist, click on the '+' button under your video, select 'Create new playlist', choose the name for your playlist, and click on 'Create'. To add more videos, simply use the same button but instead of clicking on 'Create new playlist', choose the already existing one to feature your videos there.

# Chapter 12 - Converting Your Followers

Producing a steady stream of relevant, quality content, and doing everything in your power to ensure it's the kind of information your target audience is interested in, is a key step for a successful social media marketing campaign. However, content creation is not the ultimate goal, but only a means to a goal which is conversion. You can have the best content of all, but if you don't take care of the activities to maximize your conversions, your commission rate will never come close to your total views.

If you want to reach or beat the average, follow these tips:

**Define your goals**

The first thing to understand is that there may be more to a successful marketing campaign to bring the right person to your page. Your interests could be a variety of things: generating more mentions of your brand, improving your social media presence, improving your ranking on the major search engines, improving your newsletter methods, creating more leads for sales, or simply increasing your website traffic for additional advertising revenue. If you want to boost your business regardless of your goals, you will need to properly track your results. Fortunately, there are metrics to track your goals, whatever they may be. If you're looking to increase your search engine rankings, then there are many SEO tools that can help you track your ranking in real-time.

**Create your "Buyer Personas"**

To maximize the conversions of your content, you need to be even more specific. The secret to success is to create what is known as "buyer personas" by studying their lifestyle, emotions, behaviors, age, and more.

To create the "buyer personas," you need to use all the data you can collect from your users. Go through them and try to figure out what types of patterns emerge; you need to strive to be as accurate as possible during this phase in order to segment your audience and target the part that interests you. Things like employment type, gender and age are all good starting points, but you need to find more precise characteristics. Here are some of the questions you should be asking your users:

What is their lifestyle, and how does it affect their purchase choices?

- What kind of family does my user live in?
- Who makes the economic decisions?
- What might lead them to choose my competitors?
- What are their preferences?
- What are their interests?
- What do they dream about?
- What are their aspirations?

One of the main reasons for the "buyer personas" is to be able to remember that behind every number and every percentage that we are going to analyze, there are real people with dreams, hopes, emotions, and goals. This deep approach allows for direct communication with them and will make it easy to generate the type of content they are looking for and will respond positively to.

## Increase engagement

From a study conducted by Forrester on posts made by 249 brand profiles, it was found that the best brands post on average 4.9 times per week. You have to study your niche and your target audience, you have to do some research and some work, but you won't regret it also because communication platforms are available at no cost. It is very important to know your audience and the time slots in which they are online since the most popular social media such as Instagram, give higher priority to posts with more engagement than history.

To increase engagement, use high-quality content that is consistent with your brand. When a follower of yours receives a personal shout-out from you, it will only solidify their engagement and push them to continue following you, and most likely, they could become an ambassador for your brand. Turn an emotionless relationship into a deeper connection. This way, other fans will be inspired to come up with great content, and voila, you yourself will have even more great content and supporters.

## Maximize your conversion

The final goal of everything you post on your site is to sell your products. As such, it's important to formulate your posts in such a way as to ensure that you convert as many viewers as possible into paying customers.

Additionally, it's important to always include the type of person the product in question is intended for; this will get people who are that type of person interested because it says the product was created with them in mind. Assuming that the group in question has a positive association, you will also attract people who want to be identified that way.

Declarer doesn't imply the benefits of the product in question: A recent study found that simply by listing five bullet points related to the benefits of using their service, a major online booking site was able to increase their conversion rate by nearly 200 percent.

The benefits you're talking about don't have to be revolutionary or even far outside of what you'd expect; the most important thing, though, is that any benefits you list must be real and verifiable.

## Avoid ad fatigue

If you run the same advertisement for too long can become boring to your audience, who will stop responding. You can try different time periods, but changing your ad completely or changing the offer every week or two might help. You need to prevent your audience from starting to ignore your ads because they think there's nothing new, so find new ways to stimulate your audience. Using video, humor, or an irresistible sale every now and then can help regenerate your ad.

## Match your style to your brand

The style of your ads should match the existing style of your brand. For example, if you used "skin like silk" to refer to your skincare products, then this terminology should also be made evident in your Instagram ad for those products. You need to post periodically and stay active on social media. A regular and consistent stream of content is how your audience knows you're always on and where they keep up to date with your latest and interesting business offerings.

## Use the power of Instagram

Instagram is very powerful and has some unique features, including Boomerang and Layout, that offer an amazing opportunity to showcase your products in different exciting ways. Try experimenting with them and see how you can use them to your brand's advantage.

## Imagine before you publish

Stop and think about how your ad will look on a smartphone. Social media are heavy platforms, and almost all of your viewers will see your content mainly on their mobile devices. Imagine how your ad will look on these devices and do everything you can to optimize it before you publish.

- Check the right image size.
- Check the video aspect ratio specifications.
- Remind to include closed captions.

## Highlight your call to action

The best way to get people to take action is to capture their attention. If your ad has a call to action, put it in the middle of your page, where it will show up well. This is helpful in attracting interested viewers who are already watching your video as well. Calls to action at the beginning of videos only had a 3.25% conversion rate, while calls to action placed at the end of videos were at 10.97%.

## Try Google AdSense

The first thing to do is to choose the available block formatting types to find the one that best matches your site. According to Google, the shapes that usually see the best results are 160x600, 300x250, and 336x280. It's important to respect a color scheme for the ad that doesn't contrast with the rest of your site. The location of the ad is also important because if the potential customer sees the ad too quickly, they could easily be turned away from your site. So, the least intrusive locations are usually the left or right of the sidebar.

If you're interested in trying Google AdSense, you can download a plugin to easily set it up from the plugin installation menu.

Once the plugin has been installed, simply find the list of plugins and choose the option to activate AdSense. You'll then need to visit the plugin's settings menu and choose the Get Started option (you'll need to log in to your Google account).

## Choosing Your Approach

Once you have determined what your goals are on social media, you will need to decide what your overall social media approach is going to be; after that, you can get into platform-specific strategies. Choosing your approach includes understanding how each social media platform works, how it is best used, and how it can fit into your general goals for attempting to build your business through social media. You are going to learn about how you can create an overall goal for your social media approach in this chapter.

## Learning the Benefits of Each Platform

The first thing you need to understand is how each platform is meant to be used when it comes to social media marketing. You will learn more about each platform's statistics and uses in their respective sections of this book. Before that, a general understanding of what each one offers will help you to determine which one will be most useful for your business.

For example, Instagram is a great social sharing platform for visual marketing and visual storytelling because it involves several features that are excellent for showing people your brand. You can use the picture-based profile, stories, live videos, and IGTV to show your brand to people both professionally and more intimately so that people can get a feel for who you are and feel like they are being taken behind the scenes in your brand.

Facebook is another visual storytelling platform, although it also includes personal profiles, business pages, post-sharing features, and status updates which can all be used to amplify your brand through written storytelling. Many people will use Instagram and Facebook together, as these two are owned by the same parent company and can be integrated into many ways that make each of them far more valuable.

YouTube is great if you are interested in sharing videos. It can easily be integrated with most other platforms through sharing and embedding videos. If you have a lot that you want to teach, show, or share, using YouTube to design your videos and share them can be a great opportunity to produce professional-quality videos to integrate nearly anywhere on the internet.

Twitter is primarily status updates. Although recently, they have made it more picture and video-friendly and even added a live video feed to platforms. That being said, the biggest benefit behind being on Twitter is being able to engage in conversations with people on the platform and get your brand in front of people through conversation.

Pinterest is considered essential for anyone who runs a blog, as it allows you a great amount of outreach. The Pinterest community tends to be very into DIY and picture-based inspiration, so sharing on this platform gives you a great opportunity to be seen by people who are looking for inspiration or information. Unlike other platforms, Pinterest is more of a picture-based search engine. However, it still operates as a social media platform due to the ability to message others and share Pins with people seamlessly through the platform.

LinkedIn is another great platform, especially if you are a professional who offers services over products. The system offers many ways for you to connect with people who offer services similar to yours, as well as people who are looking for the services you offer. If you build your profile properly, you can become well-established in the online business and get recommended to many different clients who may be looking for exactly what you offer.

## Deciding Which Two or Three Fit Your Needs

In order to decide your overall social media approach, you need to decide on two or three platforms that are going to suit your needs for social media marketing. Although you can certainly market across many platforms, most people find that attempting to market across too many platforms is overwhelming and can leave you struggling to generate real engagement on any of the platforms. Of course, if you have a social media marketing agency, you can always leave this up to them. The reality of it is that it will still be easier to concentrate your efforts and resources on just two or three platforms rather than several.

The best way to determine which platforms to use depends on your social media goals. If you know that you want people buying your products more, using visual storytelling platforms like Instagram, Facebook, and Pinterest will support you in visually getting your products in front of people. Most people would rather see what they are looking to buy rather than simply read about it, which is why this strategy works best.

If you are looking to talk about and promote your professional services online, you need to be looking into using platforms that are more based on the written word. Depending on what your services are, you may also benefit from having a more visual-based platform included as well. For example, if you are a marketing agency, building a following on Instagram is a good way to prove that you know how to use this popular marketing platform, and it will also help you better engage with your target audience. Aside from that, focusing more on platforms like Facebook, Twitter, and LinkedIn will be more effective for most professional services.

If you are sharing personal services, you may want to "hang out" where people hang out online, which typically includes Facebook, Instagram, and YouTube. Here, you can share pictures, status updates, and videos about the services that you offer and connect more closely with the people who are going to be most likely to actually invest in your services. The same goes if you are offering in-person services or products. You need to get in front of people and show them your location and why they need to come and visit you in person.

Ultimately, you will need to decide what platforms are going to blend best with the goals that you are trying to achieve and then get yourself on those platforms. Again, refrain from stretching yourself out too thin. Each of your platforms will come with its own learning curve as you discover how to use strategies that actually work on it. Furthermore, it is easier to gain engagement and traction on two or three platforms than it is to attempt to do it over several. If you concentrate your efforts, you will find that getting online and making a big impact relatively quickly is quite simple, which will allow you to go big and make financial progress through social media.

**Risks to Avoid**

When you get on social media, it is important that you understand that your success is not guaranteed just because you created an account and shared a few posts. When it comes to social media, many businesses are trying to reach the same audience as you are, so you need to make sure that you stand out in the crowd. The market is far from being "tapped out," but if you come onto a platform without knowing how to use it effectively, you are quickly going to get overlooked as your audience favors brands that come in with a strategy.

In this chapter, you are going to learn what risks to avoid when using social media, in general, to ensure that you are not wasting your time using the wrong growth strategies online. You will learn what mistakes to avoid on each specific platform later, but for now, it is important that you understand the general risks to avoid so that you can have a massive impact online from day one.

## Overstretching Yourself

Every single social media platform comes with a learning curve that you will need to endure in order to discover to master the platform and begin earning a high return on your social media marketing efforts. Regardless of whether or not you have already been on the platform, if you are not yet used to using that platform for marketing, you will need to learn how to adjust your approach and ensure that it is optimized for marketing so that you can increase your earnings. When you are looking to use social media for marketing, it is important that you do not overstretch yourself, as this can lead to not having the required attention to enduring each learning curve and actually putting that platform to use.

To avoid unnecessary stress, start by being honest about how much time you have each day to master your social media. If you have very limited time during the day or a few hours per week, it may be ideal to start out on the platform that is most likely to earn you an income. Then grow from there so that you are giving yourself enough time to thoroughly understand each platform. Once you have understood that first platform, then you can go ahead and start branching out to others so that you can master those as well.

Although you may want to grow big online quickly, it is important to understand where the balance lies when it comes to your growth. That is, it is a lot more productive to go big on one platform at a time than it is to spread yourself so thin that none of your platforms gain traction, and you miss the mark on every social media site you try. You will find that you master each platform and grow a lot more quickly this way, making it easier for you to start generating great success online relatively quickly.

## Spending Time on the Wrong Platforms

Another big risk that you might make online is spending time on the wrong platforms or targeting the wrong parts of the platforms. If you are not directing your time and attention properly, you can quickly get drawn into taking actions that are not productive to your overall goal, which leaves you at risk of wasting a lot of time without a lot of results.

Just because you may personally prefer one platform over another, or you may personally feel like one is better suited to your business compared to another, does not mean that this is actually the best choice. You need to be where your specific audience is and position yourself directly in front of them, or you are going to find yourself falling flat on your face online.

This way, you can ensure that you are focusing entirely on areas that will support you rather than areas that will not.

**Not Embracing the Learning Curve**

When people get on social media, one of the biggest disservices they can do for themselves and their business is to fail to embrace the learning curve that comes with being on social media for marketing purposes. If you get on social media and fail to embrace the learning curve or try to do everything your way, you are going to find rather quickly that this is ineffective and that you are going to struggle to succeed online. While you certainly do need to embrace authenticity and freedom of expression online, failing to understand the basic concepts of how to get seen and heard online will only result in you struggling to grow your business.

The learning curve can take a few days, a few weeks, or even a few months, depending on how much time you invest in social media and what you are doing to learn about the learning curve itself. If you want to accelerate this time, reading books like this one and paying attention to regular algorithm changes, new releases, and platform updates is a great opportunity to make sure that you are learning everything there is to know as quickly as possible.

Aside from consuming the information, you also need to practice putting it to work online so that you can ensure that you are aware of both what the information is and how it works in practice. The more you read, learn, and integrate social media strategies online, the faster you will be at getting your business out there and for an online impact.

That being said, make sure that you are not going too quickly online, either. If you change your strategy too frequently, no matter what platform you are on, you will find yourself struggling to stay seen because people will grow confused with what it is that you are trying to achieve. You need to be willing to give each strategy the time required to allow it to accumulate reasonable results based on your efforts so that you can determine whether or not it worked, how it could have been improved, and what can be maintained when you start adjusting your strategies.

## Blending Personal with Professional

Finally, even if you are running a personal brand, you need to be cautious about how much you blend your personal life with your professional life. Attempting to blend your personal and professional lives too much can result in you oversharing online and muddying the face of your business. When building a brand, you have to be very cautious, especially if it is a personal brand. You need to be sure that you are not sharing information that could result in you taking away from the reputation or clarity of your business. In other words, even if you have a personal brand, keep your professional and personal lives separate to avoid having personal information leak into your business and destroy your professionalism.

Even if you are well-meaning, there will be many parts of your personal life that are simply not on-brand and, if you share them, it could result in you being seen as confusing or unprofessional. At the end of the day, even if you are sharing a personal brand, there are certain parts of your life that people simply do not want to read about or heed. The people who are following you will be more interested in the stuff that relates to them or problems they may be facing over anything else. This is not because people do not care about you but because you are positioning yourself and your personal brand as a business. You need to be prepared to behave like a business.

If you do want to have a personal online platform, make sure that you keep your personal accounts private and separate from your business accounts. You can always share your business life with your personal friends but refrain from sharing your personal life with your business connections unless it in some way makes sense to your business. For example, if you are starting a fashion blog, you can share fashion topics with your professional network but refrain from sharing about your love life or relationships unless it in some way can be tied into your outfit. If you were to wear a cute outfit on a date, for example, you could share this, but do not share about your hardships or troubles that your relationship may be facing online, as this will only lead to you being seen as unprofessional. If you want to be seen as a professional business and have the opportunity to do business like a professional, you need to behave like a professional online at all times.

# Chapter 13 - Making Your Landing Page Effective for More Conversions

One step you should never overlook is to spend some time looking at the idea of a landing page to how it works with the success of your AdWords campaign. When someone clicks on your ad, you will need to send them over to a landing page. This is basically the last place they are going to hit before they decide whether or not to take the next step and become your customer. This means that you need to take some serious time and really make a good landing page.

**What Is the Landing Page?**

A landing page is going to be some kind of page on your website where people will go to make purchasing decisions; in some cases, it can also be where they go in order to get the information needed so you can make buying decisions later.

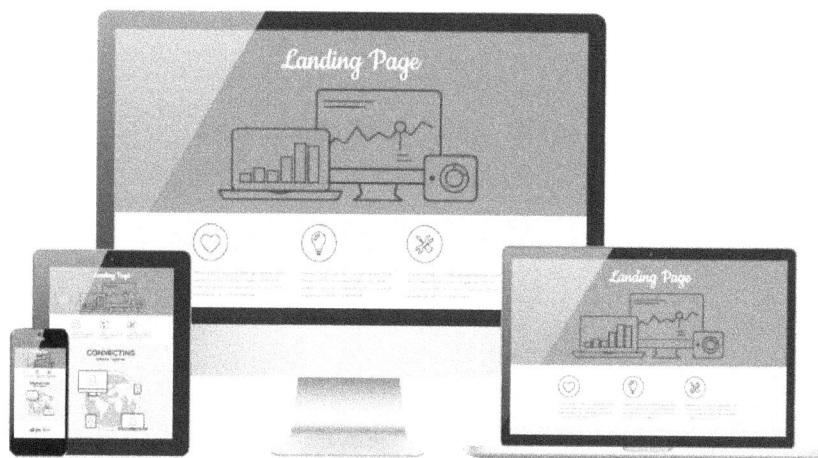

Your customer will be directed there from another website, an internal link on another page of your website, a social media link, or from one of your ads.

Landing pages should be where you are going to put the sales pitch for your product. These pages are where you will demonstrate exactly how you are going to solve the problem for your customer and try to convince them to click on the Buy button. Some of the things that you should ask yourself when considering what to add to the landing page includes:

- What do your landing pages need to look like in order to maintain the attention of your visitor?
- What do these pages need to tell customers in order to get the sale?
- What buttons, resources, and forms should be on the landing page in order to build up an email list, generate the connections that you want on social media, or make an upsell?
- How do these landing pages convey a good and positive message for your company?

**How Do You Optimize the Landing Page?**

Before you launch your AdWords campaign, you need to ensure that the landing page is optimized for the new amount of traffic that is going to flow in. You would make a major venture.

Some of the things that should be included on an optimized landing page include:

**Easy to navigate:** All of the drop-down menus need to be arranged and named in a logical manner. Contact forms and buttons should also be near the top of the page.

**Easy to scan and skim:** Use lots of bullet points, lists, and sub-headers in order to catch the reader's attention to the major concepts on the page.

**Attractive:** Try to use colors that are complementary and add in some images. You don't want to add in too much clutter, though. Put in enough to attract the customer, but not enough to distract them from the main message.

**A call to action that is obvious:** There should never be any room for guesswork when it comes to what you want readers to do on the landing page.

**Quick to offer a solution to the problem of the customer:** To sell your product as a solution, you must use this page to paint a clear picture of the problem for your customer. Explain this to the customer and then show exactly how the product is going to be the solution they need.

**Well written:** It is worth your time to have an editor look through the landing page to check for syntax, spelling, punctuation, and grammar errors. Although they might be a minor deal, they could wipe out your credibility with customers.

**Consistent with the ads:** The keywords that you added to the campaign should also show up on the landing page. Also, make sure that the same vibe, feel, and look are found on the landing page and the ads.

Avoid hiring outside help if you are trying to do everything on a tight budget. But in reality, hiring a professional web designer to create or at least look through your self-made website can help. This ensures that you are able to improve the page as much as possible in order to get the sale.

The quality of your landing page and the relevance of the keywords that you pick are going to play a huge role when it comes to calculating your Google Quality Score. Take the time that is needed in order to set up the website in a way that ensures it will generate sales.

To ensure excellent results, make sure that the landing page is going to be attractive logically laid out and that it has all of the pertinent information that your customers will need to purchase from you.

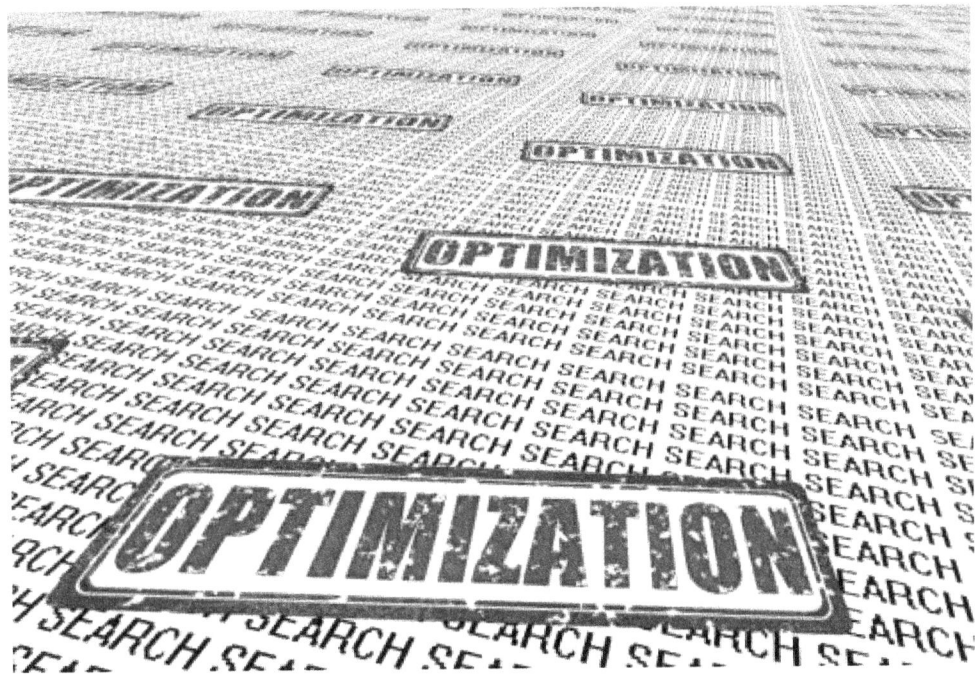

# Chapter 14 - How to Optimize Your AdWords Campaign

Now, when you look at AdWords, you know that several strategies can optimize the return that you get on your investment if you are advertising it. Mastering these tools to fine-tune the campaign and ensure that you are dialing to your specific target audience will take a bit of time for you. Sticking with it and being a bit picky with your ads optimizations can help you to get the most out of your campaign at the end. Let's take a look at some of the steps you can take to help optimize your AdWords campaign.

**AdWords Extensions**

There are a variety of extensions that you can use to customize the information that shows up in your ads. These extensions will change the layout and the look of your ads, depending on which one you choose. You have to figure out what data is the most important to some of your potential customers. Then you can use one or more of these options to get as much traffic as you can out of the campaign you work with.

There are several extensions that you can use. These extensions will include:

1. Callout extensions: These are nice because they allow you the chance to highlight the unique selling points about your product. These will be brief phrases that will appear below the description lines in your ad. They won't be linked, but they allow you to show some of the crucial aspects of the company right inside the ad.

2. Location extensions: These extensions will allow you to target your ads to a certain radius around their business location. Alternatively, you can choose a specific geographic area where show your ad. In addition, if you have a physical address, this extension will make it easier for the customer to know

exactly where they need to go if they want to shop in person.

3. Sitelink extension: This one will create space underneath the primary ad for links to other pages that may be housed on that same website. If you think that sending the customer over to other pages on the same website would serve a good purpose as well, then this is something you should consider. For example, if you are working with shoppers you know are not yet at the bottom of your sales funnel, you know they want to do more research. Giving these customers some links to click on your website can help them do a bit of research through the rest of the website.

4. Call Extensions: These extensions make calling your business directly accessible for a shopper. You will use this to place a call button right inside the ads. Call extensions are common when you are advertising to a mobile device. When you use this kind of extension, you will pay Google any time that someone clicks on this Call button.

Google is constantly changing things up and trying to enhance its extensions to fit the needs of both buyers and sellers. The best way for you to know what extensions are available and keep up with everything is to get onto the AdWords account and look through the setup pages for ads. You never know when a new bell or whistle may show up there.

**Keep Making Adjustments to Your Chosen Ads**

Explaining all of the reports that are available with Google AdWords is something that could fill up quite a few more books overall. While we won't go through and list out all of these, there is a ton of information at your fingertips when you get started with AdWords.

Learning about and deciphering all of this data can help you make the best decisions to increase profits. You can learn how to adjust your list of keywords, update the copy in your ad, fine-tune your budgeting to get the most out of your money.

There is only a little that you can prepare for when working with an online ad. In the end, it comes down to you as the advertiser being able to find the right combination of works, both in the ads and on your landing pages, that will lead to more people clicking and purchasing through the advertisements that you decide to place.

Think of all this as more of a work in progress. You will not be able to place one ad and then walk away and do nothing while you make a big profit. Even more advanced advertisers find that they need to make adjustments and change things until they reach the right mixture of what seems to work the best for your ad and your business.

Whenever you work on an advertisement, you will find it essential to figure out ways to optimize your content as much as possible to make it more likely that people will click on your ads and make it easier to make some sales on the clicks you are getting.

# Conclusion

Google is a significant part of the internet, and there's no doubt about it. Some people even think Google is the gateway to the internet. If they need something, they turn to Google to guide them in the right direction. So, Google could serve as the guide to your business. Google has created several tools to help market your business. No Marketing strategy could be complete without Google. Most methods related to SEO have been put in place to affirm to guidelines set by Google. It is all about doing everything you can to find favor with Google search engine algorithms.

Google AdWords is, without doubt, one of the biggest of them all. You must pay extra attention to AdWords because you can reap benefits from what it has to provide. Google AdWords was built from the ground up for internet marketing. Most websites that offer internet marketing services were derived from Google AdWords.

It is the fastest and most efficient way to get your page to appear on the first page of results for your targeted keyword. If you want to hit the ground running by attracting customers to your business, you should spin Google AdWords.

Google Maps can help you put your business on the map. These days we all use google maps to navigate any place we wish to go. When you claim your business on Google My Business, you can place it in front of people. Google will automatically recommend your company when they are in the vicinity based on their location. When they search for a product or service provided by your business, Google will lead them to you with the help of turn-by-turn navigation. They can also call your business or visit your Website without leaving Google's main page.

These and many more tools, which Google provides for almost free, can be used to build and grow your business. The strategies provided in this eBook will help you get the maximum results from Google Marketing. Besides AdWords, most of the tools mentioned in the eBook do not cost a penny. Hence you would not need to break the bank to present your business to your audience.

We wish you the best of good fortune and prosperity. We hope you use the power of Google to lead your business to places it has never been before.